The Evolution of the United States of America

The rise and fall of a nation

by
Richard Castagner

Table of Contents

Note from the Author

This book provides an important look at the evolution of the United States of America. It is broken into five parts: the prehistory and history of our country, an analysis of the major changes in the last 50 years, where the United States of America is now, and what the future will be for our nation.

So what is an accurate picture of America today? In the history of the world, only two nations have been founded entirely upon a monotheistic religion: Israel and America. In examining the history of both nations, many parallels are evident, namely that both were settled by those freed from a land of slavery and oppression, both were founded by a set of ideals based upon the Rule of Law rather than the rule of men (or kings), and both were greatly blessed and soon grew incredibly prosperous.

However, after achieving vast prosperity, both nations became deeply divided between the pagans (or liberal seculars) and those who held to the faith and principles of their founders, especially in the USA. After becoming divided, America lost its place of prominence and is mocked and ridiculed from within and by all her neighbors.

The pagan liberal ideology has greatly infiltrated the institution of religion. Essentially, the church has been ushered out of the public arena and told to shut up, go home, and mind its own business, when formerly it was, in fact, minding its business by educating the hearts and minds of its citizens. Liberalism has managed to almost still the voice of the church, or at least embarrass it into silence. They have marginalized the church when it should be at the very heart of our society, where it formerly once was.

I recognize that our time to win the hearts and minds of the American people is indeed short. We have no more than a decade to save this country from liberalism or socialism.

A marvelous trust, a country like no other in the history of mankind has been entrusted to us. A country where we have had the freedom to grow and thrive, to be free to achieve our full potential, to shape the futures of our children and grandchildren — that is what is at stake. Freedom of speech, one of our most sacred trusts, is already being taken from us; in its place is politically correct speech, where some minorities can say anything they want without censure or condemnation. A country where all members of mankind are recognized as equal, but certain minorities are protected and have heightened rights — is this the intended heritage of our Founders? If we fail to do our duty, we shall be judged much more harshly than any other country in existence, because we have had so much more delivered to us for which we will be held accountable.

Why must we fight? Why must we win, beyond the fact of maintaining the trust delivered to us? We have no place left to go.

In past times of human history, there were places in the wilderness to flee to. "Give me your tired, your poor, your huddled masses yearning to breathe free . . . I lift my lamp beside the golden door!" Remember those words inscribed on our Statue of Liberty? They came here for many reasons, among which were the many forms of freedom: freedom to work for yourself and your family, not the government, freedom of religion, freedom of expression, freedom from want, etc. Now, there is no undiscovered place on Earth to find real freedom.

Our choice at this point is simply to overcome the evil besetting us or to be overcome by that evil ourselves. Let these words ring in your ears and throughout your mind and spirit; if we do nothing, if we leave the fight to others, we will be overcome and many of you will live to see it. If we do not win politically, it might even reach the point where it descends into armed conflict; one has to also account for that real possibility. Do we dare wait for that conflict? I shudder to think of a second civil war, being fully educated about the savagery of the first with its far fewer lethal weapons than are available now. However, it is certainly one of the plausible scenarios that loom on the horizon.

We are being pushed toward one of three ultimate endgames: a conservative reversal of the Nation at the ballot box, the imposition of a socialist state, or a second Civil War.

We have fostered an entitlement society to the point that the poor believe they have the right to be provided for whether or not they work, whether or not they have illicit children, and no matter how they conduct themselves.

We have destroyed the Black middle class, which was thriving in the country until the introduction of the "government trough" programs in the 1980s, and has created a permanent dependent class that the liberals seek to also bring the Hispanics into. One wonders cynically whether that was about helping people or whether it was simply about creating perpetual rule for one party as they continually advance their aims.

"There is a dark cloud looming on the horizon of America. I do not pretend to be able to see beyond the looming dark cloud. I do know that a field of battle is before us. Our young people may not want to die on fields drenched red with blood, but they must battle in the classroom, in the lecture halls, at the ballot box, on Wall Street, in mass media, in the newsrooms, in the hospitals, and in the churches. They must battle at home and abroad and we must help them. We must battle not just for the finances of this nation, but for its soul.

Our people must see the need to push conservative social values or those of us who see what is at stake must go elsewhere, because the moderates and liberals in the Republican Party, with the entrenched establishment, will take us the same place as the Democratic Liberals will, just not as fast." [1]

What shall be our future? We are coming to a crossroad in our nation: either capitalism, socialism or another civil war. It may be that we shall end our forefathers' experiment with our Constitutional Republic based on a "Constitution" and a strong religious foundation.

Only time and the American people can tell.

In-depth analysis and information on the subjects covered in this book can be obtained through eight other books I have written; called the "Evolution Series".

This Series includes the history that has been revised or removed from our National Education System to facilitate Liberal Socialist indoctrination.

The book list is located in the "Notes" area at the end of this book.

[1] Clark, Charles N. (2012). Liberalism: A Subversive Force (Kindle Locations 1425–1429.

1. Prehistory of the United States of America 30,000 B.C. to 1400 A.D.

Prehistory and history are the interrelated record of human beings; each requires the decoding of different symbols and materials. History based on written documents only covers roughly the past 5,000 years.

Over one million years ago, human history started in Africa, considered the "Cradle of Civilization". Creationism, science, or extraterrestrial colonization – I will leave that discussion to the scholars.

<u>30,000 B.C. to 10,000 B.C. The earliest known period for inhabitants of America.</u> The floor of the Bering Sea between Alaska and Siberia emerged as dry land multiple times during the Pleistocene glacial advances, approximately 30,000 B.C. to 10,000 B.C. During this period of the great glaciers, this land mass was known as Berengia. A flat land mass believed to have consisted of tundra, it expanded to almost 1,000 miles across, depending on glacial flow, or narrowed to 100 miles in width. The glaciers caused the seas to lower. When the glaciers melted, the water contained in the ice flowed back into the seas, and Berengia would disappear under the ocean. This happened multiple times during this period. Human migrations took place over thousands of years. These early residents, sometimes called Paleo-Indians, traveled along the natural ice-free corridors that existed between glaciers. They hunted mastodons and other big game animals of the Ice Age — great mammoths, giant bison, large stags. They also gathered wild plants and fished. Eventually, they spread inland across North America, crossing to the Atlantic Coast; they also migrated southward into Central and South America. The earliest human record in North America is hearth charcoal found on an island (Santa Rosa) off the California coast, dated to 30,000 B.C. The California coast

ocean level during that time, the glacial period, was 300 feet lower, and thus today, coastline archeological sites survive only on islands.

12,000 B.C. to 7000 B.C. Paleo-Indian Era (Stone Age culture) The earliest group of human inhabitants of America lived in caves and were Nomadic hunters of large game including the great mammoth and giant bison. Stone Age sites were located all over North America in all areas not covered by glaciers.

10,000 B.C. to 7000 B.C. The final Ice Age. Throughout North America, glaciers began to melt. Berengia totally disappeared under rising oceans. The melting marked the end of large-scale migrations from Siberia. Over the next 3,000 years, the climate changed dramatically, with corollary shifts in vegetation and habitat for big-game species. Many of the big mammals gradually became extinct, and Indian bands based on hunting big game like the great mammoths had to shift their settlement patterns. (Scholars debate whether the big mammals died out from climatic changes or over-hunting by humans.) The bones found in bison kill sites suggest that herds of bison were driven over a cliff or into an arroyo, surrounded, and killed. These bison belonged to the big mammals of the Ice Age and multiplied into enormous herds on the North American prairies as their natural predators — lions, bears, tigers — died out and before their biggest predator, man, evolved.

7000 B.C. Extreme changes in the North American climate and animal life. The Laurentide Ice Sheet retreated as far north as the Great Lakes. As the ice retreated, the climate warmed, the tundra transformed into grassland prairies, and flora and fauna changed. Mastodons, great mammoths, giant bison, small prehistoric horses, and other mammals of North America began to die out. Evergreen (conifer) forests became deciduous with leaf-bearing hardwood trees. In the warming temperatures, woodlands spread from the Atlantic Coast inland to the

11

Midwest. North America evolved into the land that the Europeans found in the 1400s.

Climate change has been around for a very long time.

1300 A.D. The Native American population. Before the Europeans arrived, the American Indian population estimates range from 10 to 45 million people in South America, 10 to 30 million people in Mexico and the Caribbean islands, and 10 to 25 million people in the U.S. and Canada.

Linguists speculate that at the time of the European invasions in the early sixteenth century, some 400 different languages were spoken in North America.

As of 2016, a total of 566 Native tribes are recognized by the Bureau of Indian Affairs (BIA) of the United States (many more are extinct).

Despite the widespread impression that Native peoples lived by only hunting, the indigenous peoples of the Americas shaped their societies around agriculture and highly inventive horticultural techniques, which were often supplemented by fishing and hunting. The laborious processes involved in gathering and germinating roots and seeds, and finding ways to store foods, formed a crucial part of the knowledge and technologies of these early Indian cultures.

1400 A.D. European colonization (invasion) started.

The colonization period was an invasion and many terrible things were done in the process, but we must also keep a perspective.

I am not justifying the actions of the Europeans in any way but throughout history: slavery, killing, and genocide have been a normal part of one civilization

12

conquering another civilization. As American Andrew Jackson said in the American Civil War, "To the victor belongs the spoils."

The difference between the invasion of the Americas and previous world invasions was the eventual rise of the Marxism-Socialism-Progressivism-Liberalism political movement. Founded by Karl Marx in the mid-1800s, it arrived in the US political scene in 1901 during the presidency of Theodore Roosevelt. This political group, currently called the Socialist or Democratic Party, fuels their movement in part with the guilt associated with the colonization process, especially the slavery issue. The irony of this choice is that the American Indian suffered much more than the Black during the colonization period. This slavery guilt is part of the modern socialist powerbase, and they use it well to their advantage but not to the advantage of the unity of our nation.

2. Early History of the United States of America

"Early America was all about discovery and frontier. Mid America was around production and automation. Current America is around equality and kindness. Future America as it currently is heading, looks bleak, similar to the Greek and Roman downfalls and it has taken less time to get there — why?"[2]

_____

[2] Hartman, David (2012). *The Downfall of America* (Kindle Locations 70–73).

America in the Late 1400s

Before 1492, contact between North American people and the outside world was limited. Several theoretical contacts have been proposed, but the earliest physical evidence comes to us from the Norse or Vikings. Norse captain, Leif Eriksson, is believed to have reached the Island of Newfoundland circa 1000 A.D. They named their new discovery "Vinland." The only known Norse sites discovered in North America were at L'Anse aux Meadows, Newfoundland and Labrador in Canada. The Norse colonies were later abandoned.

The Viking voyages did not become common knowledge in the Old World, and Europeans remained ignorant of the existence of the Americas until 1492. As part of a general age of discovery, Genoese sailor, Christopher Columbus, proposed a voyage west from Europe to find a shorter route to Asia. He eventually received the backing of Isabella I and Ferdinand II, Queen and King of newly united Spain. In 1492, Columbus reached land in the Caribbean area.

The "discovery" of America in 1492 is a misnomer. The arrival of the Spanish in the lands that came to be known as the Americas was an invasion, not a discovery. And the invasion went quickly. The pattern was established at the beginning. Once he arrived in the Caribbean, Columbus immediately began gathering Arawaks (the local Indian tribe), whom he described as "the best people under the sun, with neither ill-will nor treachery," to take back to Spain to sell in the slave markets. It would take less than five decades for the Spanish to make the native Arawak population virtually extinct and to replace them and their labor with Black slaves brought in chains from Africa.

John Cabot discovered the continent of North America in 1497. Sailing from Bristol, England, Cabot crossed the North Atlantic and reached the coast of America, north of Nova Scotia. Like Christopher Columbus, John Cabot thought North America was India or China. He claimed the land for England.

A Portuguese sailor named Vasco da Gama discovered the actual sea route from Europe to India in 1498, around the Cape of Good Hope in South Africa. Thus, in Europe, da Gama's discovery clarified that Columbus had not discovered part of India and that calling the indigenous people "Indians" was a misnomer.

For various reasons, including the mistreatment of the native Indians and the Spanish colonists under his governorship in Hispaniola, in 1499, Christopher Columbus was arrested, put in chains, returned to Spain, and stripped of his titles and wealth. He died in obscurity in Spain.

America was named after Amerigo Vespucci, a Florentine living in Seville, Spain, who determined by two voyages around 1500 that the new lands were not part of Asia, but a new world.

America in the 1500s

In order to understand what constitutes successful colonization, it is important to understand what colonization means. Colonization refers to large-scale population movements, where the migrants maintain strong links with their former country, gaining significant privileges over the inhabitants of the new territory. When colonization takes place under the protection of clearly colonial political structures, it may conveniently be called settler colonialism. This often involves the settlers entirely dispossessing earlier inhabitants, or instituting legal and other structures which systematically disadvantage them.

Initially, European activity consisted mostly of trade and exploration. Eventually, Europeans began to establish settlements. The three principal colonial powers in North America were Spain, England, and France, although eventually, other powers such as the Netherlands and Sweden also received holdings on the continent.

The Spanish settlements started Europe's colonization of the Americas. They gained control of most of the largest islands in the Caribbean and conquered the Aztecs, gaining control of present-day Mexico and Central America. This was the beginning of the Spanish Empire in the New World. The first successful Spanish settlement in continental North America was Veracruz in 1519, followed by many other settlements in colonial New Spain and Spanish Florida.

America, and the people of America, raised all sorts of questions in Europe. Spain confronted them first. What rights did Spain have to claim and exploit the country that Columbus had found in its name? What rights did the people who lived there have that Spain must recognize and respect? What privileges did Spain have in relation to other seafaring nations that might follow and compete? Seeking answers, the Spanish crown appealed to the only supranational power in Europe, the Pope. A series of pronouncements and diplomatic initiatives from the Pope became known in international law as the Doctrine of Discovery. Designed in part to clarify the power of Christian "princes" over the lands of non-Christians who might come to their attention in the future, and in part to prevent bloody conflicts between competing princes, the doctrine of discovery authorized any such prince to exercise dominion over any territory not already subject to the claim of another Christian prince. In the 1490s, the nations most actively engaged in long-distance commercial exploration into non-European waters were Spain and Portugal. The right of discovery did not distinguish between Europe and the rest of the world; rather, it separated the Christian from the non-Christian world, the judge in this case being the Pope. In return for the right to possess, exploit, and dominate America, the Pope expected Spain to bring its people into the Christian fold.

By the late sixteenth century, both France and England had rejected the right of discovery as inadequate. Eager to exploit the riches of America themselves, they demanded a modification, which became in international law the right of conquest. Their point was not necessarily actual military conquest, but rather dominion. The Spanish could not legally claim a country that they did not occupy and control. Preoccupied with its holdings in Central and South America, Spain chose not to seriously challenge the actions of France and England to carve out claims in North America.

Thus, the right of discovery, modified later by the right of conquest, became the legal basis for the invasion and occupation of non-Christian America by the forces of the Christian princes of Europe. As the successor to the claims of all three imperial powers, the United States holds the lands within its borders by the same rights of discovery and conquest.

Upon the arrival of the Europeans in the "New World," native peoples found their culture drastically changed. As such, their affiliation with political and cultural groups changed as well; several linguistic groups went extinct and others changed quite quickly. The names and cultures that Europeans recorded for the natives were not necessarily the same as the ones they had used a few generations before, or the ones in use today.

Far from settling a virgin continent, Europeans from the very beginning moved into preexisting Indian villages and followed Indian trade routes into territories using Indian guides. From the moment of contact, the appearance of White men raised complex choices for native leaders. What the natives did not realize until it was too late was that European Christianity made it impossible for the Europeans to view the Indians in a way that allowed for fair or equitable negotiation. They saw Indians as savages, as a people without a culture, valuable only as a source of slave labor.

The Spanish priority in South America was the extraction of wealth and taking it back to Europe. In contrast, the Europeans arriving in North America (the British, the French and the Dutch) were primarily interested in settling; they wanted to develop this place as their own home. Their interests directly clashed with those of the Native Indian resident population.

Moreover, there was a clash of attitudes in relation to land. The European settlers arrived with the firm intention of owning land. However, the Indians of North America were semi-nomadic. During the spring and summer, they lived in villages to grow their crops. In the winter, they hunted in the thick forests. Land, from the Indians' viewpoint, was a communal space, impossible to own. The question of land eventually led to appalling conflicts, with the Indians the inevitable losers.

In the early 1500s, the beginning of the slave trade directly from Africa to the New World was established with slave markets in Haiti. In the next 250 years, more than 10 million Africans were shipped to the Americas as slaves.

Europeans determined rather quickly that the Native American Indian was not going to be their source of cheap labor. Native Americans, especially males, because of cultural reasons (free spirit, family structure, pride, etc.) would not adapt. This necessitated bringing in the Black slaves from Africa. The downside of this situation for the Native American was that Europeans also had come to the conclusion that the Native American was disposable.

America in the 1600s

The myth must be exposed that America was a wilderness continent filled with savages, where Europeans had to fight their way west on a continually moving "frontier." Europeans actually invaded from all directions at once. The Spanish came up from the South, the French came from the North, the Russians were coming from the West, and the English and Dutch came from the East — and guess who was in the middle.

"From a European point of view, the 1600s could be characterized by the struggle to make Indian allies in order to claim their lands. From an Indian point of view, the 'American Wilderness' was actually a highly complex ecology of peoples, cultures, wildlife and trade. The intricate pattern of relationships between all living things and their environments began to undergo fundamental and radical changes."[3]

The first successful English settlements were at Jamestown (1607) (along with its satellite, Bermuda, in 1609) and the Pilgrims at Plymouth (1620), in what are today Virginia and Massachusetts, respectively.

The Pilgrims rewriting of history was very obvious. The English, without Indian help, would not have survived that first winter, but the English credited their survival to the power of the Mayflower Compact, God's will, and their innate European superiority. The "savages" had instructed them in learned English on how to farm, fish, hunt, and construct shelters. The Indians also invited the Pilgrim colony to their annual Harvest Ceremony, which became our holiday of Thanksgiving.

---

[3] Nies, Judith (2012). *Native American History*, Random House Publishing, New York, p162.

The first colonial African slaves were sent to Jamestown and the Virginia Colony in 1619.

The first French settlements were Port Royal (1604) and Quebec City (1608) in what are now Nova Scotia and Quebec. The fur trade soon became the primary business on the continent, and as a result, transformed the indigenous North American lifestyle.

Rivalry between the European powers created a series of wars on the North American landmass that would have a great impact on the development of the colonies. Territories often changed hands multiple times. Peace was not achieved until French forces in North America were vanquished at the Battle of the Plains of Abraham at Quebec City, and France ceded most of her claims outside of the Caribbean.

The end of the French presence in North America was a disaster for most Native nations in Eastern North America, who lost their major ally against the expanding Anglo-American settlements. During Pontiac's Rebellion between 1763 and 1766, a confederation of Great Lakes-area tribes fought a somewhat successful campaign to defend their rights over their lands west of the Appalachian Mountains, which had been "reserved" for them under the Royal Proclamation of 1763.

Peter Minuet (Dutch) traded 60 Dutch guilders (about 24 dollars) in 1626 to the local Indians for the island of Manhattan (New York), although he did have to buy it again from another tribe who claimed hunting rights on the island.

The first Indian reservation was formed by English Puritans in 1630 in Connecticut. An agreement was forced on the local Indians (Wappingers), which took all of their lands and moved them to 1,200 acres, and included a long list of restrictions.

America in the 1700s

In the 1700s, most Native American people still lived in their natural environments and hunted, fished, and grew crops. For Native Americans, there was no such thing as wilderness. For the Europeans, the forest was wild, uncivilized, uninhabited, and unproductive.

In the 1700s, the Native American people of North America were primarily influenced by having to choose alliances with either France or England, and secondly by local or regional entities trying to take their lands — by agreements, cessions, or theft. The geopolitical struggle was between England and France; the local struggle was between Indian nations. Many Indian nations sided with the French who were perceived to be interested in mostly trade, while the English were land hungry and intent on settling endless numbers of colonists. No matter what side the Indians chose, by the end of the 1700s, they still lost.

By the end of the 1700s, Indians were also decimated by war, removal, slavery, disease, economic deprivation, and missionary issues. In most areas, Indian populations had been reduced by two-thirds. The next big movement building was to remove all Indians from their lands, setting the stage for the Reservation Period.

The misfortune of the American Indian tribes was not that they were a dwindling race, nor a weak race. Their misfortune was that they had held great expanses of rich lands.

With the Treaty of Paris of 1763 in their pocket, the British seemed to be masters of all they surveyed in America. However, it was precisely mastership that proved to be their undoing. The British wanted to rule the colonies remotely from

London, while the Americans wanted self-government. They had already created local law-making assemblies.

There was another rub between London and America: London tended to treat America as a useful supplier of raw materials and as a captive market for its own manufactured goods. Colonialism was still an English doctrine. The colonists' trade with other countries was either taxed or simply prohibited. Until 1763, the British enforced their regulations lightly. However, from 1764, they did it with a heavy hand, intent on raising revenues for the defense of America itself. The British themselves were almost bankrupt from the last war with France. So it was that the British passed the Sugar Act of 1764, which put stiff duties on imported molasses. This done, the British then introduced the Stamp Act of 1765, which ordered that revenue stamps be fixed to all printed documents circulated in the American colonies. This was a major mistake, for it garnered the anger of the most vocal, literate, and powerful of the colonists – newspaper publishers, lawyers, merchants, and clergy. It was from the lips of such people that first came the call of "No taxation without representation." If the colonists were not represented in the British Parliament, they could not lawfully be taxed by it.

At a meeting of colonial representatives in New York in 1765, it was agreed that they would reply to the Stamp Act by enacting a boycott of British goods. The British subsequently yielded and repealed the Act. However, Parliament maintained the right to tax the colonies and tried again in 1767, and once more backed down, with the exception of a tax on tea. The crisis came on December 16, 1773, when Boston patriots, half-heartedly disguised as Indians, dumped cargoes of tea into the harbor. Thereafter, the logic of conflict was inescapable. Britain was punitive, and America was incensed by London's "tyranny."

On September 5, 1774, a Continental Congress of 55 delegates from 12 of the 13 colonies met in Philadelphia and requested that George III remove the "Intolerable Acts." After some saber-rattling, open fighting broke out near Boston on April 19, 1775 between colonial militiamen and British redcoats. With the war underway, the colonists steeled themselves to break the umbilical cord.

In the summer of 1776, Thomas Jefferson was selected by a committee of the Continental Congress to draft a declaration of independence from Britain. The document was revised by the committee — which included Jefferson, John Adams, Benjamin Franklin, Robert R. Livingston, and Roger Sherman — before submission to the Continental Congress on June 28. On July 2, the Congress voted for independence. The Declaration of Independence was adopted by the Continental Congress and released to the American public on the 4th of July, 1776.

A number of the founders sacrificed immensely for their actions in founding America: land, fortunes, and health – even lives.

For a long, dark while, however, independence seemed a ridiculous hope, as British forces persistently routed the Continental Army of George Washington. The winter of 1777–1778, in which Washington's men spent starving and shivering at Valley Forge in Pennsylvania, reduced the Continental Army to 8,000 troops. Yet they endured and remained on the field, and time (plus a useful alliance with a provident France) was on the American side. A rash mistake by the redcoat commander, Lord Cornwallis, cost the British the war: he allowed the Americans to hem him in on land, while a French naval squadron under de Grasse blockaded him by sea. On October 17, 1781, Cornwallis surrendered at Yorktown.

By the new Treaty of Paris of 1783, the British recognized American independence, and the United States' northern and western frontiers as the Great

Lakes and the Mississippi River. As colonies, the states had been united mainly by antipathy to British rule. When that went, so did their cohesion. The colonies jealous guarding of sovereignty made central government unworkable.

Not until 1787 did the states agree upon a constitution, one that gave the federal government exclusive power over war, commerce, and diplomacy. The United States Constitution also established the executive power of the President, a Supeme Court and a Congress consisting of two houses – a Senate and a House of Representatives.

The Framework of Our Constitution

Decentralization of Government:

Because power residing with the people is a basic premise of democratic government, the government should be kept as close to the people as possible. This can be accomplished by establishing a small national government and strong local and regional governments. In a decentralized government, the constitution, and not the national ruling party, is supreme, and it should only be amended with the consent of the local and/or regional governments.

Constitutionalism:

A government of liberty is a government of laws, not of rulers or of the majority. In a pure democracy, a simple majority (just over 50%) of the people rule, and the rights of the minority could be in jeopardy. Therefore, the best form of democracy is a constitutional democracy, in which the law is supreme and protects the rights of all people. A constitution defines and limits the power of government.

Separation of Powers:

A difficulty in forming any government where people are over other people is that the government must first be enabled to control the governed, and then it must be ensured that the government controls itself. People tend to abuse power, especially if they are given too much. It has been said that power corrupts and absolute power corrupts absolutely. Due to this tendency toward abuse, the power of our civil rulers must be limited. Tyranny results when legislative, executive, and judicial powers are all accumulated in the same hands of one, a few, or many.

Trial by Jury:

There is freedom in a society that guarantees that neither life, liberty, nor property can be taken from the possessor until a dozen or so of his countrymen pass their sentence upon oath against him. Government becomes arbitrary without such a system of justice.

Civilian Control of Police and Military Forces:

Military and police power is a necessity in society to protect citizens from foreign and domestic enemies. The American statesman, Thomas Jefferson, said that "the supremacy of the civil over the military authority" is an "essential principal" of democracy. Private citizens should be able to own their own weapons, thus giving everyone the ability to defend themselves from armies that have become pawns of the government.

A Free Market Economy:

The components of a free market economy are the basic necessities for any country that desires to secure individual liberty and economic productivity. In fact, a free market economy is a natural result of the ideas of liberty. Components of a free market economy include private property rights, individual enterprise including small businesses, and a free market. The basic idea of individual enterprise is that citizens should be free to keep the rewards of their individual labor. Then, free markets prosper and the nation prospers. This assumes fair and limited taxes and an honest banking system.

Election of Representatives:

29

Frequent elections are essential, and it is vital that the elections be free. This means that individuals who run for office should be able to do so without restrictions, winning the race in the free marketplace.

With a good government founded, America resumed its relentless westward expansion. Spurred on by the Northwest Ordinance of 1787, which both blueprinted political organization for new territories and sold Indian lands cheaply (at a dollar per acre), settlers poured by the thousands into the land between the Appalachians and the Mississippi.

In the same year, America ensured her westward future in the greatest real estate deal of all time. Tiring of her possession of Louisiana, Spain had sold the entire land to France, who was persuaded to part with it cheaply by the guileful President Thomas Jefferson. For 800,000 square miles, Jefferson paid $15 million. To put it another way, Jefferson paid three cents per acre for most of the West beyond the Mississippi. The Louisiana Purchase, which doubled the size of the United States, had another useful aspect. It removed the possibility of French interference in the new nation.

America in the 1800s

By 1812, America and Britain were at war again in what, for all intents and purposes, was Revolutionary War II. As John Quincy Adams noted, the United States had no alternative but war "or the abandonment of our right as an independent nation." The ensuing three years of conflict were bloody but inconclusive, and both sides slinked to the negotiating table at Ghent. Little was given and little was asked, save for a mutual ceasefire. However, the 1814 Peace of Ghent brought an era to an end. Britain at last gave up her imperial ambitions toward America.

"The 1812 War finally shrugged America free of the colonial interference of Britain. Henceforth she would be mistress of her own ship. In case anyone was in any doubt, the fifth president, James Monroe, fashioned a Doctrine in 1823 by which the USA disbarred European powers from colonization in the Western hemisphere. The Monroe Doctrine became the guiding light for US foreign policy thereafter; all the 'international' wars the USA would fight for the next century would be wars — Mexico in 1846, and Spain in 1898 — to stem or reverse Old World imperialism."[4]

America's splendid isolationism in world affairs allowed her to direct attention to some colonization of her own – the settlement of the American West. From 1843, there were major overland migrations to Oregon, and in 1845, Texas became the 28th state of the Union. It seemed, in the phrase of the year, the

---

[4] Lewis, Jon E. (2012). *The Mammoth Book of How it Happened – America* (Kindle Locations 6914–6920).

"manifest destiny" of America to rule the northern continent. Proof, if it were needed, came in the discovery of gold at Sutter's Mill, California, in 1848, which began the great gold rush, and thus brought California into the Union. Yet, for all the glittering allure of gold, the big bait out West was land for farming. It mattered little that the West was already occupied by the Native Americans; in the name of manifest destiny, they were killed or relocated. In only a handful of years after 1843, the number of White people living in trans-Mississippi America vastly outnumbered the 350,000 Native Americans there.

Ironically, it was America's very success in the conquest of the West that provided the pretext for the Civil War. While some western states were admitted under the Northwest ordinance of 1787, which forbade slavery, others were admitted under cobbled-together compromises such as the 1854 Kansas–Nebraska Act, which allowed some states to maintain slavery. Faced with the Act and the Dred Scott decision in the Supreme Court in 1857, abolitionists in the Democratic and Whig parties split to found the Republican Party. In 1860, the Republican candidate, Abraham Lincoln, was elected President. The irony of this situation, the Democrat Party owned the slaves, the Republican Party actually freed the slaves. With the possibility of slavery being constitutionally abolished, South Carolina seceded and was joined by six other states in forming the Confederate States of America in February 1861. (Four more states joined later.) On April 12, Confederate forces began the bombardment of the federal arsenal at Fort Sumter, South Carolina. The Civil War had begun.

Four years later, almost to the day, on April 9, 1865, in the silence of Appomattox Courthouse, the Confederate army of General Lee surrendered. During that time, over 600,000 soldiers died of wounds and disease, and much of America, from Virginia to Arkansas, had been reduced to a battlefield.

The American Civil War was a particularly bloody conflict. In Pickett's charge at Gettysburg, 8,000 (60%) soldiers died in a single attack. The bloodiness was caused in part by the passions involved, and in part because of the advanced technologies available – mass-produced rifles, artillery, battleships, and even machine guns. The American Civil War was the world's first industrialized slaughter. Consequently, the North was always going to win. The North had more factories, a better rail network, and more people. In addition, in 1862, the North began the enlistment of Black soldiers. At its peak, the Union army was one million strong; the most the South could put into gray was 500,000 men. The price of victory was high: Lincoln himself was assassinated, while the South, to ensure it obeyed the abolition of slavery, was placed under military occupation and coerced into democracy.

That effort failed when the last troops were withdrawn from the South in 1877. Southerners created "Jim Crow" laws, which imposed segregation of the races. Not until 1954 would segregation be banned by the Supreme Court. Even so, the Northern victory allowed the reunion of the states and the continued westward march of the American Empire.

The 30 years after the Civil War were the great decades of the "taming" of the West, the spanning of America from sea to shining sea with ribbons of rail, and the transformation of the Great Plains into the world's most lavish beef butchery and bread basket. More American soil – 430 million acres – was occupied and placed under cultivation between 1870 and 1890, than in the entire two and a half centuries since the landing at Jamestown. Effectively, by 1890, America had colonized its own West. The last gasp of the free Plains Indians had come at Wounded Knee, and the census of that year could find no meaningful "frontier" between the wilderness and the zone of settlement.

Freely able to exploit the agricultural land of the West, along with its vast reserves of raw materials (oil, coal, iron ore, and timber being principal among them), American industry was able to grow at a stunning pace. One measure will serve: in 1865, production of steel ingots and castings was less than 20,000 long tons; by 1898, it had reached 9,000,000 tons. By 1900, the United States was producing 23.6% of the world's manufactured goods, even more than the United Kingdom.

To labor in America's factories, millions of immigrants were siren-called across the Atlantic. Between 1860 and 1890, the population of America doubled, from 31,443, 321 to 62,947,714. Such a population was good for laboring and good for the business of buying, but not quite good enough for the hyper-efficiency of US industry. Goods needed to be sold abroad, and pushes to "open doors" in foreign lands were urged on the government. Under such pressure, inevitably enough, American foreign policy changed from isolationism to imperialism: the new compass direction for manifest destiny was abroad. By 1900, the signs were there for the world to see: America had the money, the people, the guns, and the self-belief to be a superpower. Most Old World nations had already recognized America's new status; in 1892, they upgraded their representatives in Washington, DC from mere ministers to full-blown diplomats.

America in the 1900s

To astute observers, this was clear at the outset, the dynamism of the American economy was in place.

Theodore Roosevelt was as diplomatically aggressive as he was astute; he won the Nobel Prize for mediation in the Russo-Japanese War, and he oversaw a rapid buildup of the USA's naval strength. Between 1900 and 1910, America's warship tonnage burgeoned from 333,000 to 824,000. Just to make certain the whole world knew that the USA had arrived as a great power, Roosevelt dispatched "The Great White Fleet" around the world in 1907.

On the domestic front, Democrat Roosevelt was greatly influenced by progressivism (modern day liberalism or socialism), and he sought a "square deal" for labor by restricting the power of the industrial monopolies.

When his handpicked successor, Taft, turned pro big business, Roosevelt stood against him in the election of 1913, which let another progressive Democrat Woodrow Wilson slip through the middle to the White House. Wilson, even more than Roosevelt, was a child of progressivism, and "New Freedom" ideas in education, labor relations, welfare, and electoral processes did much to fundamentally change American society. Does this sound familiar?

As zealous about waving the "big stick" as his predecessors in backyard territories, he was traditionally "isolationist" with regard to spats in Europe. This suited the electorate well, and in 1916, Wilson was re-elected on a peace ticket.

Germany's unrestricted U-boat campaign, however, provoked the USA into the First World War in April 1917, where her sheer output of war material and men (a million troops) finished off Germany in 1918. Germany was defeated, and

France, Great Britain, and Russia were exhausted. The Old Order was gone. By 1918, the whole world knew that America was the Great Power. Not that she chose to play the part.

Within a year, America had retreated into collective isolationism and refused to ratify the Treaty of Versailles, which established the League of Nations. America's withdrawal from the wider diplomatic world was only confirmed by Republican Warren G. Harding's election to the presidency in 1920 on a "return to normalcy" ticket. It was business as usual in 1920s America. Her standard of living aroused the envy of the world, and more and more people – especially from impoverished Europe – fled to her shores. There seemed to be no limits to American entrepreneurship, witnessed, above all, by Henry Ford's introduction of mass production methods for the Model T automobile. Meanwhile, the stock market boomed, real estate went wild, and the immoderate whooped it up on bootleg liquor in speakeasies (prohibition had outlawed the manufacture and sale of alcohol in 1919). Some called it the Golden Age.

But all that glitters is not gold. American agriculture had long been depressed, and the consumption of consumer goods was dependent on thin credit. On October 29, 1929, Wall Street crashed. Factories closed and farms were repossessed by banks. The Great Depression was on. Within three years, 15 million Americans were out of work.

Against this grim background, the nation put its faith in the "New Deal" of Democratic candidate Franklin D. Roosevelt, elected to the White House on November 8, another child of progressivism like his cousin Teddy. Loans to businesses, price supports for farmers, and public works – notably the Tennessee Valley electrification scheme – were put in place to promote recovery.

However, it was the war in Europe, not the "New Deal," that really got the wheels of industry and agriculture whirling again, due to increased armament orders from Britain from 1939 onward. Although Roosevelt's personal predilection was for American involvement in World War II, the mood of the country was against him. In any event, Roosevelt had his way, for the war came to America: on December 7, 1941, the Japanese carried out a surprise attack on Pearl Harbor. Showing the same rashness as the Kaiser, Hitler then declared war on the United States, which totally changed the balance of forces in the conflict. As Churchill said, after 1941, the war henceforth was merely "the proper application of overwhelming force." The USA, aside from provisioning her Allies (she was producing an aircraft every five minutes by 1944), led both the Second Front in Europe and the Pacific Campaign. Only a technological miracle could have saved the Axis against US money and manpower but America had the technological miracle – the atom bomb.

Unlike 1918, the United States was determined not to retreat into post-war isolationism. Besides being a founding member of the United Nations, America also took a lead in establishing NATO (Europe) and SEATO (Pacific Rim), the purpose of which, in accordance with the Truman Doctrine, was the curtailment of communist expansion. SEATO was dissolved in 1977 due to a lack of member interest.

The "Cold War" with the USSR also shaped politics at home, with Senator Joe McCarthy leading a "witch hunt" for communists in the United States from 1952 to 1954.

There was a less obvious effect of the Cold War on the US domestic scene: military spending and the space race with the USSR, which provided the prosperity

38

of Eisenhower's 1950s. Eisenhower's tenure (traditional Republican) in the White House came to an end in 1960 with the election of Democrat John F. Kennedy to the presidency.

Something changed in America that year; some of the pall of Cold War suspicion and oppression lifted. Kennedy caught the mood perfectly in his inaugural speech, which called for a new frontier in social legislation, particularly in civil rights. JFK was a moderate Democrat but the party was starting to change. The Left radicals of the '60s were starting to take over the Democrat party. Abroad, Kennedy promoted humanitarianism (the Peace Corps) alongside traditional anti-communism; even conservatives admired his refusal to blink in the confrontation with the USSR over the latter's installation of missiles in Cuba in 1962. The life of "JFK" was cut short on November 22, 1963, when he was assassinated in Dallas.

As the 1960s rolled on, the problems on Lyndon Johnson's (JFK's successor) desk mounted; America's embroilment in the Vietnam War split the nation, and there was widespread racial unrest and student radicalism. The "Civil Rights Act of 1964" was passed. This period changed the direction of America dramatically; the Radical, Black, Indian, and Female Power Movements were born along with the associated Big Government. In 1968, both Martin Luther King and Robert Kennedy (JFK's brother) were assassinated.

Johnson decided not to seek re-election, and Richard Nixon won the presidency for the Republicans on a platform of withdrawal from Vietnam and increased law and order in America's cities, which were enduring a drug and crime wave. Enjoying the afterglow of the 1969 Apollo mission that placed Armstrong and Aldrin on the moon, as well as detentes with Russia and China, Nixon was re-elected in 1972. That election, which came with a landslide of votes, was his undoing, for during its course, White House operatives had burgled the Democratic National Committee headquarters at the Watergate complex in Washington, DC. Nixon resigned the presidency (the only President to have done so) on August 9, 1974, under threat of impeachment.

His Vice President, Gerald Ford, took the seat in the Oval Office.

To an electorate dismayed by the chicanery of politics, Democrat Jimmy Carter's liberal down-home politics seemed the ideal antidote, and he was duly elected in 1976. Already, the fingers of economic downturn were gripping the US economy, as high oil prices and cheap foreign competition decimated the traditional industries of the rust belt. Inflation reached a 30-year high in 1979, and Carter's attempt to control inflation by raising interest rates only produced a recession. Any good will Carter enjoyed disappeared on November 4, 1979, when fanatics took 66 hostages at the US embassy in Iran. The bungled attempt to rescue them sealed Carter's electoral fate in the election of 1980.

At the age of 70, former actor and governor of California, Ronald Reagan, was the oldest man to be elected President of the USA, but any doubt about his durability ended when he survived an assassination attempt in 1981. Elected on a Republican promise to restore American supremacy, Reagan proved politically durable as well and sat tight through the worsening recession. By late 1983, the economy had picked up (claimed by his supporters to be due to Reagan's supply-side economics, and by his detractors to the drop in oil prices), and Reagan won a record 525 electoral votes in the 1984 election. Unlike his presidential forbears, Reagan pursued a vigorous anti-communist stance abroad, calling the Soviet Union the "evil empire."

When Ronald Reagan (a solid conservative) was elected to office, the attitude of the country dramatically improved – almost overnight. No longer was America this bungling, inept, uncertain, aging power but a young, energetic nation once again.

Not since JFK had America been as optimistic as during the Reagan years, and those times of optimism lasted not only for his eight years in office, but for most of the three decades that followed his inauguration.

Coming into office on the heels of the popular Reagan, George H. W. Bush (a Globalist Republican) had most of his successes in foreign policy. He also handled the unexpected fall of Soviet power in Eastern Europe well, and used his diplomatic skills to liberate Kuwait in 1990.

Bill Clinton's record as President includes balancing the national budget for the last time and intervening in trouble spots, such as the Middle East and Northern Ireland, as well as committing peacekeeping troops to Bosnia and Herzegovina.

Bill Clinton was a traditional Socialist; he tried to be bi-partisan.

In retrospect, it can be seen that the 1900s was America's best century but deep structural and political changes were already in process in the last half of the century.

America in the Early 2000s

New Year's Day of 2000 broke over a happy and confident United States of America. After all, the preceding 100 years had truly been the American Century. The United States had awakened from its isolation to become the greatest nation on earth and possibly the greatest in history. During the twentieth century, America had twice rescued Europe from chaos. It defeated German and Japanese imperialism, Nazism, and Communism, while seeming to grow ever stronger. Americans followed the advice of Abraham Lincoln and destroyed their enemies by making them friends. With incredible generosity and wisdom, the United States rebuilt defeated nations and made them into democracies. In doing so, it became the world's dominant economic, military, political, technological, and cultural power.

All is not as it seems at times. The most important things in history are not events, they are processes. The death of America's Democratic Constitutional Republic was a process already underway in the late 1900s, but few people recognized it. The America of 2000 seemed so wealthy, so powerful that it simply could not fail, but the Great Republic may already have been doomed. The US was deeply in debt and losing its lead in industry, science, and education. Professional politicians and special interests were gaining total control of a large and very powerful national government and were corrupting public life. The foundations of America's strength were being eroded by five radical power movements that formed in the 60s.

"Typical Americans of the early twenty first century had many fine qualities. It is a pity that modern historians will remember them mainly for

42

their gullibility. Americans would discover that they had a very naive faith in the financial system, that the stock market did not have to go up year after year and the home they purchased for a foolishly high price could not be sold to an even greater fool. With incredible naivete, they followed 'experts' into financial disaster. Millions of individuals, corporations and banks will bankrupt and the financial system will suffer a major breakdown."[5]

The optimism of the 1990s was shattered by the 9/11 attacks in 2001 on the United States. Islamic terrorists from the Al-Qaeda hijacked four passenger airliners, flying two of them into the World Trade Center in New York and one into the Pentagon, with the fourth one crashing into a field in Pennsylvania after an onboard struggle between the passengers and the terrorists. Three thousand people were killed or reported missing.

The Bush Two presidency (A Globalist Republican, just like his father) evolved around the War on Terror following 911, and prompted military intervention in Afghanistan and Iraq.

Bush Two also had to deal with an accelerated drug war in Mexico that started in 2006 and evolved into an actual military conflict, with each year more deadly and hopeless than the last.

Under Bush Two, starting in the winter of 2007, a mortgage financial crisis began in the United States, which Obama compounded with his financial policies during his presidency, eventually triggering a national and worldwide recession.

---

[5] Gibbon, Edward (2013). *COLLAPSE: UNITED STATES HISTORY 2000 to 2050* (Kindle Locations 230–233).

I have always wondered about the timing of this financial crisis, just before the 2008 election. I am also wondering about the timing of the Covid crisis that happened just before the 2020 election.

Obama was elected president in 2008, the first radical Socialist as a President. Obama's determination to "fundamentally change" America meant he would seek to redistribute income through expanding socialist welfare programs (the ideology of victimization) to the detriment of the middle class. Obama would fund a dramatic expansion of the federal bureaucracy with burdensome tax increases, often buried within programs such as a nationwide program of government health care (Obamacare) that Hillary Clinton had failed to pass in the first year of the Clinton administration.

Obama would divide the nation economically and racially, such that Obama's rhetoric would seek to divide the rich and the poor, with the result the United States would experience not a "post-racial" world in which poverty would be eliminated, but an economically weakened America, deeper in debt than ever in our history, with the a resurgence of economic envy and racial hatred such as the United States has not experienced since the post-World War II era.

"Obama's radical socialist position on race was on the verge of rekindling a race war in the United States with racial violence that has not been seen in the streets and communities of America since the dark days of the 1960s race riots. Ironically, the first president of Black descent brought forth an era of renewed racial conflict." [6]

---

[6] Obama Nation II: Judgment Day" by Jerome Corsi, 2015, Kindle loc 236.

44

Crafting a foreign policy to the detriment of Israel, Obama would unilaterally reduce the military strength of the United States, while engaging in a foreign policy designed to reduce the influence of the United States in international affairs and to substantially reduce the US military.

Even worse, Obama doubled the US national debt in his eight years in office and presided over an anemic "economic recovery" in which millions of American workers have abandoned the labor force altogether, in a job environment where the vast majority of new jobs created were part-time, and minority unemployment in the Black community persisted with record highs. Meanwhile, some one half of US families was on taxpayer-subsidized food stamps. The work requirements of the Clinton era welfare reforms were eliminated, and many Democratic-controlled cities, such as Chicago, Baltimore and Detroit were bankrupt.

The glow of the "Hope and Change" and "Yes We Can!" slogans that propelled the Obama election in 2008 lost their glow quickly.

> "For Obama, truth was secondary to a socialist ideology that condemns America as a racist, imperialist, colonial nation, regardless of the steps the United States has taken to abolish slavery and eradicate racism from our hearts and minds, in the spirit of Dr. Martin Luther King, who had urged Americans to judge a person not by the color of their skin, but by the quality of their characters." [7]

In 2016, the Trump presidency was an unexpected surprise to the Socialist Movement. Trump derailed their plans for a socialist takeover of America, although the derailment may be temporary.

---

[7] Obama Nation II: Judgment Day" by Jerome Corsi, 2015, Kindle loc 237..

Trump (a Populist Conservative) created an immense and loyal base that stressed maintaining America as it was founded, a Constitutional Republic with the emphasis on the Constitution, God and individual freedoms.

There was an unbelievable contrast between Trump's term and the past Obama years, continuing with the pending Biden years.

Obama was taking America down the road to Socialism, but to install Socialism he had to destroy the America we know, and then replace with Socialism. Biden now is being manipulated by the Obama machine to continue these Socialism goals.

Trump was trying to maintain the integrity of our Constitutional Republic. His accomplishments during his "America First" doctrine were monumental. There was not a single area of our Nation that he did not have positive influence on, including protecting the American "Constitution".

His major presidency accomplishments are listed in the Notes at the end of the book.

This was the large problem to the Socialists! Trump interfered with replacing the "Constitution" with a Socialist totalitarian government. They (Socialists, Democratic Party, Rhinos and many establishment Republicans, Left Stream Media, Hollywood, special interest groups, public unions, high tech companies and social media, imbedded socialists in the government and the court systems, etc.) persecuted and tried to impeach him three times during his term and then removed him from continuing his second term with a suspect election. The American election process has been totally corrupted by the Socialists.

Research the processes that happened during late 1900s to Argentina and Venezuela. The same process is happening right now, the political transition from Capitalism to Socialism, in America.

Biden became president in 2020. He is a moderate socialist but his agenda is being controlled by radical socialists including Obama handlers with Islamic influence.

The future does not look good for our Constitutional Republic.

The coming decades will be a battle against Socialism and Islam to keep our Constitutional Republic.

God help us!

For more historical detail see the "Historical Timeline of the United States of America" at the end of the book.

3. United States of America in the Last 50 Years

The nation's character is being terribly wounded from within by moral confusion, widespread immorality, abandonment of commitments, and negligence of our families, homes, churches, and schools. America is not only being torn apart by her own leaders, but by her own people: us.

Moral character begins with individual virtue, which builds nations, but individual immorality tears them down. America's moral character is but a shadow of what it once was. Until roughly 50 years ago, Americans' sense of what was right and what was wrong was quite clear and consistent. There were such things as moral absolutes, and most Americans agreed on what those moral standards were. Much of America's moral standards were based upon the Bible, but now those standards can't even be read, spoken, or heard in our public squares and schools. In the past, the majority in society set the moral standards, but now the minority prevents any such standards from taking hold, especially through the tyranny of Socialist power tools.

Throughout America today, moral absolutes have been replaced by moral relativism: "What's right or wrong for you isn't right or wrong for me." The decline in moral standards and the rise in moral relativism did not occur suddenly, which would've likely been recognized and subsequently defeated. It is only by looking back to where we came from that we can see how far we've declined. As the standards in our society have crumbled, immorality has increased to the point that we can barely even recognize it for what it is. We seem trapped by our own inability to identify what's right and what's wrong. And even when we can identify it, too many of us are too afraid of "offending someone" to speak out.

As immorality increases, so does the size and scope of government that is needed to contain such evil and countermand the effects of immorality. As Americans have traded their individual religion for the liberal secular state, they are starting to realize what previous generations intrinsically understood: with sin comes tyranny.

Like the Roman Empire and other infamous civilizations that fell, the American Republic will collapse under the weight of her own immorality — unless we dramatically change course.

For the past century, America's broken moral compass and rising tide of immorality has been responsible for creating most of the cultural and national problems that are now overwhelming us. Our declining national character and our collapsing civil institutions are intrinsically joined – as one decreases and declines, so does the other. And as our problems increase and our civil institutions collapse, more liberal, authoritarian government institutions are needed to combat our lack of self-governance and rising dependence.

For the last 50 years, too many Americans have come to believe that larger government, more money, and more education will solve our problems, but they have only continued to make them worse. Whenever there's a problem in education, defense, or energy, the immediate answer from Washington is to haphazardly throw billions of dollars at it and hope it goes away before the next election cycle begins.

Economic inequality will become the defining issue of the time and a major cause of our Great Republic's death. This inequality will fall most heavily on those young people of the early twenty-first century as they are crushed by unemployment, high taxes to pay the government debt (incurred by their parents, not them), and the increasing costs associated with a liberal socialist "Entitlement Doctrine." No modern society can function for very long without a healthy middle class or at least the promise that one is quickly developing. When a majority of people decide that tomorrow will not be as good as today, the system is doomed. Sadly, this crisis may very well be by design, a process to accelerate our transition to a socialist nation.

As faith in the American Dream dies, so will the Republic's future; it is only a question of time.

When a civilization collapses, it usually doesn't happen all at once; it is merely the grand finale after a long period of decline, of rampant immorality, a loss of national identity, and a lack of purpose. If America is to endure, we must rediscover who we are as Americans and what made America a truly extraordinary country.

Five Movements that are radically changing US Democracy

These five Major Movements in the last 50 years have had major changes on our Republic. All of these movements are related to the influence of the Radical Movement in the 60s.

1. The transition from Capitalism to Socialism Movement
2. The Islamization Movement
3. The Female Power Movement
4. The Black Power Movement
5. The Indian Power Movement

1. The transition from Capitalism to Socialism Movement

In the 1960s, the new left (liberals) seemed to emerge from nowhere. In the United States, during the late 1950s, church attendance was on the rise and the conservative Young Americans for Freedom was the most rapidly growing student organization on many college campuses. In the early 1950s, conservative, liberal, and radical social theorists agreed that American students were basically conservative and supportive of the American social and political system. No one predicted the rise of a radical student movement.

With the advantage of hindsight, we can now point to changes in American society that foreshadowed the emergence of the New Left, changes that were both brought about and encouraged by the civil rights revolution and, perhaps more importantly, by the Vietnam War. In any event, beginning with the Port Huron Statement, while the ideology that permeated it resembled that of the Parisian Left Bank of the 1920s and 1930s, the combination developed by the New Left was unique.

Almost from the start, the New Left hurled a dizzying array of challenges at the American social and political systems. This antiestablishment ideology encompassed a rejection of "politics as usual," political and social institutions, of social tradition and sexual mores, and even of Western culture itself.

It contained within itself, as one sympathetic commentator noted, elements of anarchism, socialism, pacifism, bohemianism, mysticism, and black nationalism. Indeed, the list extended far beyond that, including tendencies toward communitarianism, syndicalism, Maoism, and other similar movements as well. Some radical youth seemed to combine nearly all of these tendencies within themselves, almost schizophrenically.

Initially, the white segment of the student left was heavily middle class and Jewish in background, as were its adult supporters. The young people who made up the New Left were often the offspring of successful liberal or radical parents. By the late 1960s, however, the composition of the movement had changed. Non-Jews from conservative backgrounds (in genuine rebellion against their parents) joined it in large numbers, as the Students for a Democratic Society (SDS) and other radical groups grew rapidly.

What were the '60s about? And why has that decade so strongly influenced American life? All four of the major power movements that changed our Republic started during this timeframe.

At the time, many critics traced America's disorders to particular events, such as the war in Vietnam or the race / gender issue. Marxists and neo-Marxists, on the other hand, perceived them as reflecting far deeper crises in the capitalist society. The most widely read theorists of the period, however, were a group of writers who concluded that the student activists were a new breed coming into their own as the result of changes in cultural and child-rearing patterns. The motives and values of radical youth were seen as products of being raised by upper-middle-class professionals who held secular and liberal or radical social outlooks and who employed permissive child-rearing techniques.

A traditional ideology of free market capitalism rests on the assumption that the greatest good arises from each individual freely pursuing his own chosen activities. The ideology of free-market capitalism assumes that each individual knows best what is in his economic interest. Each individual, then, ought to be free to pursue those economic ends. The central value of the more traditional view is economic freedom, rather than economic equality.

The liberal ideology of free market capitalism is the aggregation of all individuals acting in pursuit of their individual private goods within the rules set by the community to regulate human activities. Traditional liberalism called for economic freedom within a framework of emotional and expressive restraint. The new liberalism discards expressive restraints but adds economic controls.

Liberal Democracy and Capitalism in Europe emerged out of a particular cultural and personality matrix. During most of human history, most people in Europe lived in tightly controlled communities or under authoritarian regimes. They still do.

We therefore suspect that the politics of most Western societies will, in the future, be characterized by increasingly intense, and perhaps violent, ideological conflicts, and that the existence of democratic order in such societies will become increasingly a problem. This is already becoming apparent with the Muslim lack of assimilation today.

Born during the 60s radicalism period by Saul Alinsky, the liberal indoctrination process involved eight levels of community control to transition from capitalism to socialism:

1) Healthcare: Control healthcare and you control the people.

2) Poverty: Increase the poverty level as high as possible; poor people are easier to control and will not fight back if you are providing everything for them to live.

3) Debt: Increase the debt to an unsustainable level. This will produce more poverty.

4) Gun control: Remove people's ability to defend themselves from the government so that a police state can be created.

5) Welfare: Take control of every aspect of people's lives (food, housing, and income).

6) Education: Take control of what people read and listen to, and take control of what children learn in school.

7) Religion: Remove the belief in God from the government and from the schools.

8) Class warfare: Divide the people into the wealthy and the poor or black and white. These divisions will cause more discontent, and it will be easier to tax the wealthy with the support of the poor.

Do these eight steps look familiar? The socialists are incorporating these steps into our democracy to "fundamentally change" America from a Constitutional Republic to an authoritarian socialist state.

Socialism, Feminism and Black Culture Power Tools:

Socialism, Feminism and Black culture power tools must be redefined or eliminated: like feminism, racism, multiculturalism, political correctness, woke, cancel culture, victimhood mentality, affirmative action, sexual harassment, equity and equality, etc.

Feminism:

Feminism has manipulated human nature; they know it is easy to get people to identify with victimhood. The standard feminist motto is "equal rights for women." The problem is that feminism is not about equal rights at all; feminism is about political power for the socialist feminist.

Females are told they must free themselves from the male patriarchal society. They must make work a priority, be independent, not need men, not have children and not support the nuclear family. Females should become Alpha Females; gender independence, be more like the male thus males will not be needed. One of feminisms major mantras is that men and women and boys and girls, are the same, except for some basic plumbing.

Males are left out with the exception of his checkbook. Sadly, most males today are not and in many cases, cannot be involved directly with raising and teaching their children.

The female in our current Western Society is being fast-tracked to success and is getting enormous financial and emotional support. Life for the female today is marvelous until they hit adulthood and figure out they are not happy, with or without children. Feminism has given them a lifestyle in conflict with their basic biology. They are unhappy and angry, who else to blame but that patriarchal male. Male emasculation is a natural product of this process. The irony, although males today have been basically neutered, is they are still being accused of toxic masculinity.

Adult males today are adjusting as best they can today. The main concern is young boys.

Young boys are the victims growing up today in a feminist dominated society where young girls are supported and perfect but young males are defective. Many young boys are getting frustrated, are seeing the tough road it is going to be to stay a traditional male and are opting for gender fluidity, etc. They feel they are fighting a losing battle trying to stay a traditional biological male.

Parent or parents; you can spend your life raising a wonderful, well-balanced male who is comfortable with his gender but as soon as the child hits our education system, he is totally reprogrammed (brainwashed) to the feminist and socialist ideology.

Sadly, when many males hit adulthood, they have no idea what a traditional male role is or was. Feminism indoctrination in western society has been very successful. They have created a generation of adults who totally believe that it is OK for a person to choose their gender.

What many adults today do not realize is that the decision was made a long time ago when they were young impressionable children thru an experiment per feminism that has worked well for feminism but has been a disaster for the western male and female and the nuclear family.

56

Feminism and socialism are destroying our Western Civilization.

If this process continues; the male and female relationship and the nuclear family is going to become obsolete.

Racism:

In America since the days when slavery was a profitable institution, racism has existed – as it has in most other cultures of the world. And while there was a great deal of racism in America for much of our history, because of the efforts of Martin Luther King Jr. and other civil rights leaders of the 1960s, racism had greatly declined in America.

A handful of political opportunists like Al Sharpton and Jesse Jackson combined with the socialist Democrats, discovered that America's struggle with racism could be used for their personal, political and financial gain and created the "race industry." Though only pockets of true racism remain, these opportunists regularly condemn America for her racist past and demand reparations or more redistribution of wealth (managed by them, of course) in order to pay for those past sins.

Never mind that America overwhelmingly elected a black man as President only forty years after the Civil Rights Movement. In the minds of these race-opportunists, America will always be racist and never be absolved – and of course, must forever pay for her past sins.

Another plague upon the spirit of America is the mass protests that often turn violent in our cities and their flagrant acts of anarchy and destruction.

The "Defund the Police" and "Police Brutality" movements by the socialists has evolved into a radical crime increase in our nation and police assassinations are becoming a way of life!

The protests which become violent and disorderly have no place in America, nor should those who organize and populate them. Whether such protesters are anarchists, radicals, or even teachers and professors, they should protest in a peaceful, orderly fashion in an attempt to get their message across. Violent, chaotic protests only serve to hurt their cause and distort the picture of America, as well as turn most of the informed public against them.

Sadly, socialists are divisive race-baiters and try to divide America into groups and classes and pit us against one another for political gains.

Multiculturalism:

In the last fifty years, multiculturalism has evolved in the USA, which tossed out the great melting pot and replaced it with the notion that all immigrants could not only retain their own customs, languages, and lifestyles but should not assimilate into America. Not only that, but multiculturalism and political correctness worked together, forcing Americans to change to accommodate the various sub-groups rather than those groups integrating into the existing American culture and adding their own distinct culture/flavor to it.

In the United States, the issue of multiculturalism has been largely ignored. It has either been inappropriately represented or misunderstood for years, perhaps both. As citizens, we have allowed ourselves to be convinced that diversity is a good thing for those within (and outside of) our country. In some instances, encouraging diversity is a correct and appropriate position for the citizens of our country to adopt; in others, it is not.

Do we want to live in a country where, when we travel from one community to another, we need to speak a different language? Where some communities are likely to be resentful of "outsiders"? Where cultures do not mix, are not shared, and where people have nothing in common? Do we want to allow multiculturalism to segregate our country and then wonder if it will literally come apart, as the Soviet Union and the European Union has?

If the answer to these questions is no, then we must address the many issues caused by our present attitude toward multiculturalism.

Abraham Lincoln said,

"A house divided against itself cannot stand."

Insofar as these forces divide our nation, our country is weakened. Today we see the insidious signs of multiculturalism everywhere. Unless we want a fractured and divided country where different languages are spoken, where anarchy reigns supreme, where people are pitted against anyone from a different segment of the population, where we cannot feel free or safe to come and go to other parts of the country or even to parts of our own towns, then we must recognize the dangers of multiculturalism and make the necessary changes. Either we do this, or we will continue down the path to more and more separate and individual societies, instead of building a single and solid, united American society.

Politically Correct and Woke:

I have often wondered what is correct about being politically correct. I have come to realize that the term demarks a relationship between a designated victim and an oppressor. For example, females or Blacks by law are considered designated victims. In the context of this book, it means females and Blacks are good and

Caucasian men are bad. The only correct opinions are expressed by victims—in this case, females or Blacks.

At some point in the future of our country, I hope that disagreeing with an officially designated victim stops being considered an act of oppression. It can be an act of communication. But since I am a Caucasian male, my views hold very little validity. If I disagree with politically correct, I am sexist or racist and must be reprogrammed.

What's not correct about political correctness is that politically correct hate and intolerance are permitted as long as they are not directed at any of the designated oppressed victims. The socialist Democrat strategy: divide America into victimized groups, and then showcase viewpoints that tell the victim narrative while blaming the alleged oppressors. The victim groups of choice are usually blacks, women, gays and legal / illegal immigrants. The oppressors are those bad Republicans, Christians, and white males.

The irony of this situation is that the majority of the people in our country today are legally designated oppressed victims. I tried to research the actual population percentages associated with the victim groups. The data links have been removed from the search engine data bases: Google, Yahoo, etc.

At the heart of politically correct language lies dishonesty, not civility. This reality is manifested in the preference for a vague / neutral word over literalism, for vagueness over specificity, and for propaganda over honesty, example CNN. The politically correct society is not the civilized society, but rather the dishonest society.

Politically correct does more harm than good. When people attempt to censor themselves in the interest of being politically correct, they inhibit

60

themselves from expressing the truth. When people choose their words too carefully, they often delete the truth. Real, honest dialogue is the best way to produce complete and honest reasoning about political issues affecting all people. When people are politically incorrect, some may be offended, but that is much better than censoring one's thoughts, which eliminates the possibility of expanding ideas and thinking critically about issues.

Politically correct has been harmful to society. It has inflicted on schools and universities a sort of totalitarian mentality where everyone must constantly monitor what they think or say out of fear of being declared 'politically incorrect.' Conformity to politically correct norms and orthodoxy has replaced independent and critical thinking.

Political correctness did far more than just replace words like 'chairman' with 'chairperson'. It was instrumental in dumbing down Western education. PC was based on the postmodern, mystical belief that naming something is what gives it power. PC censors subscribed to the Orwellian notion that stopping people using certain words destroys whatever it is the word signifies.

What does it mean to be woke? Those who consider themselves woke, even if they don't use the label, might see wokeness as an embrace of positive virtues, such as tolerance, fairness, awareness and fighting racism. The reality, "wokeness" is racist, they are what they say they are fighting.

Woke or wokeness is essentially PC on steroids.

Political correctness and Woke are both without question harmful for the future of any democracy.

Cancel Culture:

There is no single accepted definition of cancel culture, but at its worst, it is about unaccountable groups successfully applying pressure to punish someone for perceived wrong opinions. The victim may end up losing their job or is significantly harmed in some way well beyond the discomfort of merely being disagreed with.

Most victims of cancel culture are generally not powerful people. They are often vulnerable people who suffer devastating harm.

In no way is contemporary cancel culture about free speech or debate. Nor is it any longer primarily about social justice. The power to get someone fired must be a thrilling feeling.

What is harder to understand is why the truly powerful, those with the power to suspend and investigate and to fire people, are allowing this? Perhaps they fear becoming targets themselves. Whatever the reason, there is no denying that cancel culture exists and is getting worse.

Sadly, the cancel culture is also being used to destroy our nation's history unless it's socialist history.

Victimhood Mentality:

Following the Civil Rights and the feminist movements fifty years ago and the subsequent implementation of socialist affirmative action policies, it has become commonplace for entire groups of people to be portrayed as victims of society. Sometimes there are legitimate victims, but most people claiming such victimhood status today are not; they're simply trying to blame others or "the system" for their own problems.

But who cares if we are becoming a culture of victimhood? We all should. To begin with, victimhood makes it more and more difficult for us to resolve political and social conflicts. The culture feeds a mentality that displaces the necessary order of give and take—the very concept of good-faith disagreement—turning every policy difference into a pitched battle between good (us) and evil (them).

The victimhood culture is power based and makes for worse citizens—people who are less helpful, more entitled, more selfish, and more destructive.

Per fifty years of socialism, our education system is producing a generation of sheeple who advocate socialism and have no real survival skills. The sad reality of this situation is that they are the long-term future of our country.

Victims and their advocates always rely on free speech and open dialogue to articulate unpopular truths. They rely on free speech to assert their right to speak. Victimhood culture, by contrast, generally seeks to restrict expression in order to protect the sensibilities of its advocates. Victimhood claims the right to say who is and who is not allowed to speak and this is totally supported by our left-leaning MSM.

On college campuses, activists interpret past ordinary interactions as "microaggressions" and set up "safe spaces" to protect students from certain forms of speech.

Does this mean that we should reject all claims of victimhood? Of course not. Some people are indeed victims in America—of crime, discrimination, or deprivation. They deserve our empathy and require justice.

Affirmative Action:

Affirmative action is one of those programs that just does not work and is impossible to administrate. The result is unqualified people advancing in organizations, being admitted to colleges, getting construction bids, etc. Affirmative action has suffered the same fate as feminism. The power pendulum of affirmative action has long overshot equilibrium. Part of the process of the male and the female getting on the same page again involves correcting this over-swing.

Why should a white person be penalized for something his great-grandparents did over a hundred years ago? We are staying locked in the failures of the past instead of embracing a truly gender and color-blind society.

Affirmative action is wrong. First of all, it is wrong to judge someone on race or gender instead of academic ability, characteristics, or other talents for college and for a job. The most qualified person, no matter what his or her race or gender, should get it.

Affirmative action violates the equal protection clause of the fourteenth amendment to the Constitution. The equal protection clause prohibits the state from denying any person equal protection under the law; affirmative action is a law that treats people unequally. Also, schools and companies should be able to choose who they want to represent their corporation. If a university wants all African Americans or a C.E.O. wants only Hispanics working for him, so be it.

Last but not least, affirmative action makes minorities seem weak because it looks like they can't survive on their own or get educated or have a job without the help of the government.

There is no way the United States should be using affirmative action anymore. It may have been necessary at the time of its adoption, but I don't think it applies any longer. It puts non-minority people at a disadvantage. In order to create a truly gender and color-blind society, we must stop treating people like gender or race makes them different.

Sexual Harassment:

Sexual harassment is a perfect metaphor for a big challenge coming up in the male and female relationship: the challenge to our genetic heritage of protecting women, the challenge to the stereotype of innocent women and guilty man, the challenge of keeping our society and workplace flexible and fluid rather than petrified and paralyzed, and the challenge to respond to sexual nuance with communication, not legislation.

If we desire to protect people from being hurt, we would also have to outlaw women's sexual rejection and emasculation of men. I think most of us would rather live in a country where we are free to make and learn from our mistakes rather than being subject to litigation for every mistake we make.

Sexual harassment legislation is sexist because it holds only men accountable. It protects women who sexually harass without protecting coworkers from her. Ultimately, it ignores the woman's role and therefore ignores women— except as a victim.

The MeToo movement was formed in 2006 by Tarana Burke, an advocate for women in New York as a forum to help women who had endured sexual violence by letting them know that they were not alone—that other women had suffered the same experience they had.

It has been a positive forum for female rape and violence but it has shortcomings. It does not address sexual violence against males very well and is very partisan to the left.

65

Equity and Equality:

Equity is a whole different ballgame. It is predicated on the idea that the only certain measure of "equality" is outcome. The equity-pushers assume axiomatically that if all positions at every level of hierarchy in every organization are not occupied by a proportion of the population that is precisely equivalent to that proportion in the general population, that systemic prejudice (racism, sexism, homophobia, discrimination, etc.) is definitely at play, and that there are perpetrators who should be limited or punished that have or are currently producing that prejudice.

There is simply no excuse for this doctrine.

Equality per equity is being championed by feminism and Socialism today, where a person is allowed to choose their gender, even children and usually male. This will be a complete disaster for society.

This can be confirmed by asking any current female athlete if she enjoys competing against biological male athletes.

Young males are subject to this pressure from early childhood because of single female dominated home environments and is reinforced when they enter the education system. Many male children are being imprinted with feminist ideology since birth and behavioral programming toward a young child is a very powerful social programming tool. This is producing a generation of young males today who not only question their gender but may not have the energy to fight feminist programming.

A human tendency for survival is to take the easiest path in life; young boys may be taking the gender fluidity path today. Rather than fight for their biological male, they are choosing gender fluidity: homosexual, bisexual, transgender, sex change operations or choosing to be a gender different from your biological gender, etc.

As free people and citizens of the United States of America, we have every right to express ourselves the way that we see fit. When those who are offended threaten a lawsuit if we don't bow to their wishes, we should inform them of our First Amendment rights and then promptly ignore them. If they take us to court and the court rules against us, then we must appeal or even not comply with the court-ruling that violates our rights. A court of men has no right to violate our natural, God-given rights, especially when those rights are enumerated and protected by the Supreme Law of the Land: the Constitution and the Bill of Rights.

Socialism, Feminism and Black Political Power Tools:

Socialism, Feminism and Black political power tools must be redefined or eliminated: like socialism (marxism), feminism, racism, big government, gridlock, socialism "free market" capitalism, education (critical race theory and common core), one payer health care system, illegal immigration, sanctuary cities, voter fraud, national crime, biased LSM (MSM), high tech, social media companies, entertainment industry and Hollywood, energy dependence, military training, globalism, etc.

Political System:

No nation was more blessed than the United States at the time of its founding. Washington, Adams, Jefferson, Madison, and Monroe would have been political giants in any age. The fact that they served as the first five presidents was impossibly good luck, but by the end of the twentieth century, America's political luck had run out. American political life was not in decline, it was crashing. The political class – the United States never had an inherited ruling class in the same sense as less fortunate nations. But even if there was no ruling class, there had always been a political class of professional politicians, bureaucrats, and hangers-on who collected around government.

One might argue that this situation had always existed, but in the twenty-first century there were several new aspects. The size and power of the American government had grown far beyond the wildest thoughts of the Founding Fathers. For decades, government in America played a relatively minor role in the lives of most people. Consequently, the political class remained small. Starting with the Income Tax Amendment, the Federal Reserve, and the Social Security Act of the

1900s, this began to change. The federal government became a source of benefits, an aggressive tax collector, and the enforcer of thousands of laws. As government involvement in all things grew, so did the political class. In fact, it grew completely out of control.

The damage done by Bush and Obama, especially the radical socialist Obama, in the early 2000s will be largely responsible for the probable fall of America. It divided and demoralized the nation as never before. It left us with a political system consisting of two uncompromising parties of blockheads. That system simply could not deal with serious problems. The economic mess and the deficit gave rise to America's angry 'Lost Generation' and it was those young people who have given up on democracy and may bring the Republic down.

No American, living or dead, has ever experienced such a prolonged period of failed leadership; the people grew quite cynical about government. Historians will look back on the Biden-Obama era as a tragic failure of democratic government. When America needed prudent, mature, and pragmatic leadership it got two presidents who were blindly devoted to the ideology of radical socialism. The political system was poisoned by outright hatred between Socialist Democrats and Republicans, while the majority of moderate Americans were trapped between two sets of self-serving political parties.

The list of government giveaways and entitlements is literally endless! These government programs have one sinister goal: to increase the number of Americans who rely on the government for everything.

This ever-expanding group of dependent Americans forms the rock-solid base of the liberal establishment. Without them, there would be no Democratic Party. The career-liberal politicians know which side of their bread is buttered and

69

will do everything in their power to expand the number of people who are dependent on the government for their well-being from the day they are born to the day when a future death panel decides they should die.

The liberal political machine can buy the votes of those who are dependent on government handouts by giving them more and more free stuff. This is the liberal motivation behind the blind support of globalism and open borders. It will be difficult, if not impossible, to curb our present ever-expanding welfare state without killing or cutting a few liberal sacred cows along the way. However, kill them or cut them we must if there is to be the slightest chance of reversing America's slide into obscurity.

It's time to change the existing political system; it doesn't work anymore. There is too much polarity between the two current American political parties, working together is impossible.

The most important issue facing our Nation right now: ELECTION INTEGRITY! We must take the country back in the 2022 Congressional Election and the 2024 Presidential Election or our Constitutional Republic falls!

Financial System:

There is a radical difference between the traditional ideology of free market capitalism and the socialist ideology of free market capitalism.

"The traditional ideology of free market capitalism rests on the assumption that the greatest good arises from each individual freely pursuing his own chosen activities. The ideology of free market capitalism assumes that each individual knows best what is in his economic interest. Each individual, then, ought to be free to pursue those economic ends. The central value of the more traditional view is economic freedom, rather than economic equality.

The socialist ideology of free market capitalism is the aggregation of all individuals acting in pursuit of their individual private goods within the rules set by the community to regulate human activities. Traditional socialism called for economic freedom within a framework of emotional and expressive restraint. The new socialism discards expressive restraints but adds economic controls per expanded government role."[8]

Everyone in America has a need for something – a cause, a need, or a way to spark new business, and many of them are asking for federal money to do it. Even the individual states are jumping on this bandwagon, like California, which is essentially bankrupt from overspending. Both parties are guilty of overspending and allowing things to get out of control, without any measures to limit it, resulting in over a $20 trillion national debt in 2019. Unfortunately, this stems back to three basic themes: no accountability for what is being spent, everyone's hand in the pot, and the American need to want everything today and not wait for it. America needs to be run like a business, not like a communist or socialist regime, which won't work and has failed throughout history, time and again.

One party is mainly guilty of entitlement overspending. The concepts of federal entitlements, welfare, food stamps, etc., to assist the needy are important, but they must be managed properly so that people are moved off them over time and become contributors to society. Otherwise, America becomes a country of leeches that feed off the success of the few. This draws the country down negative

---

[8] Rothman, Stanley. *Roots of Radicalism Revisited* (The World and I Online, 1988) Kindle loc 361–366.

paths, such as what is happening now, and people begin to question the direction of the country.

The result is that the status and presence of America as a leader in the global economy is diminished. It is wrong to believe other countries have better answers than America does, based on the success of America. If we do not reverse this negative course we have set out on, we will continue to spiral downward into a new dark age that will once again stifle the growth of all humans on the planet. Being equal and poor is not sufficient; being poor with the ability to strive to better oneself, to move up in status, is what America is all about. America is a land of opportunity, and if we are not careful, we will give that away.

Socialist democracy and capitalism in Europe emerged out of a particular cultural and personality matrix. During most of human history, most people in Europe lived in tightly controlled communities or under authoritarian regimes. Socialism was introduced to Europe rather easily.

Socialism is having a more difficult battle in the USA because of the nature of the American people under a democratic constitutional republic, but it is still winning so far.

If socialism dominates US society in the coming decades, it's a lose-lose for our country. We lose our Constitutional Republic to socialism, and we will be more susceptible to Islamic infiltration and Islam Jihad.

I can see a daughter looking up at her Caucasian mother in the mid-twenty-first century US, and after adjusting her Muslim niqab so all you can see are her very sad blue eyes, saying, "Why were grandpa and grandma so stupid?"

We therefore suspect that the politics of most Western societies will, in the future, be characterized by increasingly intense, and perhaps violent, ideological conflicts and that the existence of democratic order in such societies will increasingly become problematic. This is already becoming apparent in the Muslim assimilation, or lack thereof, into Western societies.

Education System:

An ignorant people will quickly become an enslaved people. Only an educated populace can be permanently free. What the educational institutions of a country teach lays the foundation for either liberty or bondage. In recent years, where socialists have taken over countries, one of the first things they have done is assume control of the educational system. Education must not be government-controlled; it must stay in the private sector.

Even this will not totally solve the problem; the teaching environments and the lesson content in America's education system have been taken over by socialism and feminism over the past fifty years.

In America today, even if a child may be instilled with a wonderful set of values and morals by his or her parents, he or she is totally reprogrammed to socialist ideology by the time they graduate from our educational system.

"The biggest problem with our universities is that they purposely tear down the values of the students and indoctrinate them with secular, socialist thinking. Since the 1960s, most young people go off to college with the values instilled in them by their parents, churches, and communities, and then emerge with an entirely different set of values. That's evidence of indoctrination or even brainwashing by our higher education system."[9]

Socialist indoctrination and control tools currently in our national school system called "Common Core" and "Critical Race Theory" are marxist indoctrination tools.

One of the primary reasons the American experiment has been failing over the last century is because of our negligence in passing down our American values, beliefs, history, religion, and heritage to the next generations.

When a nation forgets its heritage and history, it quickly loses its identity. This is one reason why socialists love to distort and rewrite history—because it causes people to question and doubt their heritage and heroes. Since the rise of socialism, America's heroes and Founding Fathers have been marginalized, denigrated, and even vilified in our universities and, most recently, our public schools. Lately, very little room in our history books is given to them and their incredible accomplishments, as socialist educators are in favor of providing additional room for the more recent history of the socialist era.

Traditional Religion:

Except for liberal secularism and Islam, all religions are under attack in our Republic. Life is often difficult and challenging, and it's easy to look at the world around us and feel helpless or even hopeless, especially when evil seems to be increasing. Everyone, but children especially, need regular doses of common-sense moral teaching. Our churches and synagogues used to provide these moral reinforcements, but with the rise of secularism, many people today derive their morals from whatever media and books they consume – most of which are secular or even anti-religious.

---

[9] Hambleton, Chris. *Restoring the Republic* (2013) Kindle loc 1326.

Every attempt, therefore, to remove this Republic from "under God" means that either anarchism or communism will surely result, whether planned or not, by those who strike at God's place in American life. It is an inescapable alternative.

Healthcare System:

Obamacare is failing to meet its promises of cost containment, affordability, and improved quality of care. It will never assure coverage for all Americans and is unsustainable in the long run. It has been flawed by political compromises and trade-offs from the beginning that favor corporate stakeholders in the medical-pharmaceutical complex over the needs of patients and their families.

Unfortunately, if we end up with a one-payer medical system, there will be nowhere for average Americans to go when they become ill; they will be stuck, as the average Canadian is now, with long waiting lines and, in the near future, death panels, whether they are rich or poor. Of course, as with most of the socialist policies that are being forced down our throats, exceptions will be carved out for our political leaders and the bureaucrats who work for them. Politicians and bureaucrats who are well connected will always have access to the best medical care available, at little or no cost, in medical centers like Walter Reed. That's the way it is and always will be in a socialistic society.

A major overhaul is also required in the entrenched Medical and Pharmaceutical Industries to improve efficiencies and to lower costs plus pricing. This step would have to be completed before any kind of health care reform should be considered for our country; whether a single payer or a market-based healthcare system.

Illegal Immigration (Open Borders) and Sanctuary Cities

It is important to emphasize that the millions of legal immigrants who reside in this country are not the problem and are productive members of society who work hard, play by the rules, and pay taxes.

The real problem is that nothing of significance has been done to curtail the flood of illegal immigrants, including human trafficking, drugs and potential terrorists, who cross our southern border on a daily basis because the socialist Democrats see the newcomers as future members of their socialist voting bloc and cartels see them as easy money.. Additionally, big businesses, especially agribusinesses, consider illegals to be a cheap source of labor. All of these self-serving reasons to skirt current law speaks volumes about our corrupt politicians

Sanctuary Cities must be outlawed also; they are basically are "get out of jail" cards for illegal aliens. These cities do not support ICE in the proper and legal exportation of criminal illegal aliens.

I would argue that these items only scrape the surface with respect to the price we are paying for governmental policies that are allowing large segments of the country to be literally overrun by illegals from our southern border and war refugees from the Middle East. Many of these immigrants from the Middle East may be terrorists infiltrating America to do us harm.

America must close the loopholes in a broken immigration system and secure the southern border, preferably with a wall.

National Crime:

We are paying a high price for diversity and an even higher price for not recognizing the fact that, even after sixty-plus years of money being poured into inner cities and a host of other social programs designed to lift the downtrodden minorities from poverty, the crime rate per the FBI 2012 Uniform Crime Report is many times higher now in minority communities than it was even before Lyndon Baines Johnson began his infamous war on poverty in the 70s.

The socialist press has refused to recognize the racial component of crime in the United States, and its failure to do so has contributed to the lawlessness that is pervasive in our inner cities.

The national justice system under socialism is practicing a dual approach currently; one system for socialists involving "get out of jail" cards and another for everyone else involving full prosecution.

The punishment for crimes must be made so painful that prospective criminals think long and hard before they proceed with a contemplated criminal act. We have been coddling criminals for the last fifty years, and guess what—it isn't working!

We must return to the time when spending time in prison was a painful experience. Probation would be exceptional, and judicial practices such as parole, indeterminate sentencing, and judicial discretion would be eliminated entirely. There should be a fixed sentence for every crime, and the prescribed sentences should be fully enforced without exception.

Gun Control:

Liberals have an ongoing campaign to confiscate all citizens' guns. Luckily, we have not discarded the Constitution and the Bill of Rights yet.

Military and police power is a necessity in society to protect citizens from foreign and domestic enemies. The American statesman, Thomas Jefferson, said that "the supremacy of the civil over the military authority" is an "essential principal" of democracy.

In order to ensure civilian control of the military, the President should be commander-in-chief of the armed forces during wartime. Rules including money for armies should be established by Congress (representatives of the people), rather than by the President, in order to keep the support of the military subject to the approval of the people.

The police force should be locally and regionally controlled and totally separate from military power. The heads of police forces should be elected and governed by local government. Police should be hired by the local government as employees.

Private citizens should be able to own their own weapons, thus giving everyone the ability to defend themselves from armies that have become pawns of the government.

Biased Left Stream Media, High Tech and Social Media companies:
Nothing can dampen one's spirit faster than turning on the news, picking up a newspaper, or listening to a newscast these days. "Socialism is good, Capitalism is bad" or "all white people are racist" or "all males suffer from toxic masculinity". Far-left bias has been the media's primary direction for decades. The media have discovered that the more horrific, violent, racial, and politically biased the news is, the better it sells and the higher the ratings. When people have a strong emotional reaction to something, they become more likely to purchase or view it. But what does such repetition of violence and bad news do to people's attitudes and the society those people inhabit? A steady diet of terrible, depressing, biased news soon creates the very society that once provoked it to outrage!

News media bias is real. It reduces the quality of journalism and it fosters distrust among readers and viewers. This is bad for democracy.

Many prevailing left leaning biases exist in the US news media. The Washington news media are biased toward Washington-based solutions and the mainstream political press in the US has a totally leftward tilt on social, political, and economic matters.

The leftwing bias of the American mass media is pervasive. Since the 1980s, studies have consistently shown that the professionals who constitute America's mainstream news media—reporters, editors, anchors, publishers, correspondents, bureau chiefs, and executives at the nation's major newspapers, magazines, and broadcast networks—are preponderantly left-oriented and socialist Democrat.

MSM in the US is basically the propaganda arm of the socialist Democrat Party in our Nation.

Pravda on steroids.

Bias in the news media manifests itself in the form of outright, intentional lies, and what reporters choose not to tell their audience (i.e., the facts they purposely omit so as to avoid contradicting the political narrative they wish to advance

The purpose of the media is (or at least used to be) to honestly inform the public of current events and more space should be given to local and regional news in place of national and global news. Opinion has very little relation to raw news most of the time, and the two should be kept entirely separate, which is the purpose of a news section in a paper or a newscast. Unbiased, objective reporting is what most Americans expect from their news sources, but is not what they are given today.

Biased Entertainment Industry and Hollywood:

Another significant cause of America's cultural decline comes from our national addiction to entertainment and Hollywood. Hollywood and the entertainment empires have taken it upon themselves to not only determine what American cultural standards are, but what they should be. When Hollywood's influence was confined mostly to movies, it was relatively harmless; however, after television was invented and Hollywood secured a constant presence in our lives and homes, it soon began consciously influencing our values and culture.

Hollywood and the entertainment industry are giving you a biased mix of information, and often don't even present the conservative viewpoint; they are not doing their jobs. They're not representing the interests of the American people; they're representing a minority of the population and trying to convince us that their viewpoints are the way we must go.

Class Warfare:

When Obama burst onto the national political scene at the Democratic National Convention in 2004, many saw that perhaps he was the one to finally fix the racial problems in America. After all, he appeared to be the ultimate African-American, being the son of a Black man from Kenya and a White woman from America. And by his campaign, Obama was only too happy to absorb the hopes and dreams of so many Americans in finally bringing racial harmony to the United States. But has he? Not by any measurable means. If anything, racial tensions have only worsened because of his repeated use of class warfare tactics between the rich and the poor and between the minorities and the Whites for purely political purposes.

When politicians can't (or won't) unite their constituents, they divide and conquer – which is what Obama was doing for most of his public life. He is a radical socialist; a radical socialist destroys with no intention of rebuilding. Hillary Clinton is also a radical socialist. A liberal socialist will negotiate, as Bill Clinton did during his presidency. What's truly tragic about Barack Obama is that he had enormous potential to heal many of this country's wounds, but he squandered that potential for cheap political socialist gains. Today America has not been this politically (or culturally) divided since the days of the Revolutionary War and the Civil War. We are not divided between various regions or states today, but citizen against citizen, neighbor against neighbor, and brother against brother.

For the past century, too many of our politicians have divided us in order that they might be elected into office and acquire power – to conquer us without firing a shot, to subject us to servitude without cracking a whip. Rather than seeing ourselves as Americans with our common bonds of morality, culture, traditions, language, history, and heritage, too many of us see ourselves as Democrats and Republicans, our second "Evil Twins". By their policies and actions, our politicians have successfully divided Americans into warring political parties, classes, and subcultures. But not only have we been divided politically; we are now deeply divided culturally between traditional America and pop-culture America – and as evidenced in the last election, pop-culture America appears to be winning the battle for the heart of the nation.

The Obama administration was engaged in race-baiting, knowing that rubbing raw the class conflicts experienced by a Black underclass would only intensify the political support the Obama administration could expect to receive from Black American voters.

"Obama's radical socialist position on race is on the verge of rekindling a race war in the United States with racial violence that has not been seen in the streets and communities of America since the dark days of the 1960s race riots. Ironically, the first president of black descent has brought forth an era of renewed racial conflict."[10]

There was a method to Obama's madness; as a radical socialist he wants a race war, a crisis. This would allow him to activate the National Guard and confiscate citizens' guns, another very important socialist goal.

With Obama, America was being condemned as racist, because even as President, he seemed unable to get beyond looking at skin color as an excuse to issue judgments of condemnation upon the nation that he has declared in his heart true, regardless of the facts. For Obama, truth was secondary to an ideology that condemns America as a racist, imperialist, colonial nation, regardless of the steps the United States has taken to abolish slavery and eradicate racism from our hearts and minds, in the spirit of Dr. Martin Luther King, who had urged Americans to judge a person not by the color of his skin, but by the quality of his character.

The Trump Presidency made great strides in redirecting the country back toward its "constitutional" roots but the same Socialist policies are now being continued in the Biden Presidency per the long arm of the Obama Presidency.

---

[10] Hambleton, Chris (2014). *Restoring the Republic (Our American Awakening: Book 3)* (Kindle Locations 331–335).

Energy:

Global energy independence, using both fossil and environmental sources, is a necessity in the modern world.

The United States is a world leader and the nations of the world look to the United States for leadership. American energy independence is about world leadership.

Energy independence does not mean closed borders or economic isolation. Energy independence can be achieved by producing abundant and affordable alternative transportation fuels through advanced technology that enables all countries to do the same. American energy independence was achieved by Trump and led to global energy independence.

The nation will be going back to energy dependence under the Biden administration.

The globalists and the socialists have more power when the US is energy dependent.

Military:

A strong military is paramount to the freedom and stability of America and the world. From the time America's armed forces entered World War I in 1917 until today, the United States military has repeatedly meant the difference between civilization and barbarism. It is no exaggeration to say that a militarily strong America is the one indispensable prerequisite for a peaceful and prosperous world. The witness of history, as well as our own common sense, bear testament to the fact that when America's armed forces are powerful, focused, and feared, the globe is a better place.

An Obama presidency downsized US Army, stretched too thin to fight two wars simultaneously, was judged "weak" in an annual assessment of US military power according to the Heritage Foundation's 2016 Index of Military Strength.

The declining state of the overall readiness of the force, long warned by leaders from all military branches as reaching crisis levels, was a major factor in the poor scorecard, according to the Heritage Foundation.

Readiness is also being tested by requiring soldiers to take woke socialist training.

In the twenty-first century, due to our vast wealth and technologies, we have not been sorely tested. Our beloved nation does not have a martial spirit, and perhaps does not need one. It does, however, need a strong military infused with a warrior spirit.

America has been drifting. That should scare us all.

In summary, under Obama, our enemies did not fear us and our friends did not trust us.

President trump reversed this situation but Biden will return us there.

World Globalism:

What's needed to achieve a new American global strategy is political will and a strategic vision to meet the three interrelated challenges of supporting freedom, defending the national security, and restoring our nation's economic health.

The first challenge – reaffirming the historic American commitment to freedom in the world – involves making it clear that we will do whatever we can to support people fighting for fundamental rights, although we must insist that they take financial responsibility for their own success or failure

Committing ourselves to preserving US leadership in the world is, therefore, the second major challenge for US policy. This is not an expression of American arrogance or a reckless form of overreaching. The urgent challenge now is for the US to exercise leadership in a convincing manner so that the vacuum is not filled by hostile powers or by chaos and violence.

However, continued US leadership is simply not possible unless we address a third critical challenge, which is to bring the spiraling US public debt under control. Over the last decade, the gross federal debt has more than tripled to over $20 trillion and now exceeds the total national GDP. The gross federal debt is projected to reach $38 trillion by 2024 under the socialist Biden administration. This will bankrupt the US; which is the socialist goal, ask Argentina or Venezuela how this turned out!

While there are many reasons for the continuing surge in public debt, including the 2008 fiscal crisis and the wars in Iraq and Afghanistan, the principal factor has been socialist spending and Covid costs. Unless we can summon the political will and bipartisan consensus to reverse our domestic decline, no amount of strategic vision will enable the United States to exercise the kind of leadership that the world so desperately needs.

The Trump presidency was very successful in overcoming all of these challenges during his term until Covid entered the picture just before the 2020 elections, very suspect timing.

The United States may not be able to develop a grand strategy; indeed, in a world of ever-increasing complexity, perhaps the mere desire to attain one is unrealistic. What is certain, however, is that US foreign policy will grow more incoherent the longer it postpones a candid discussion on its role in the world.

The socialist crisis-driven foreign policy was inevitably going to succumb to disorientation and exhaustion. The United States needs to have a serious discussion about its role in the world – one that matches objectives and means.

The US needs to establish some new rules for dealing with the World countries in the political and economic areas. We should not be the World's policeman any longer and should stop paying countries to be our allies or friends.

Globalism is not the answer to a good world. Nations should take of their own citizens first.

The challenge we face today is as great as any in American history. Our national security and the values we cherish, in addition to the future of democracy in the world, rest on our ability to rise to this occasion.

2. The Islamization Movement

Religion, especially the rise of Militant Islam in recent years, is in the news, media, and a topic of diplomacy in international politics. The post-911 world has, in my opinion, given Samuel Huntington's "Clash of Civilizations" thesis a renewed sense of urgency.

The major problem with the desired approach by the religions in America to stay out of politics is that it is not the approach being used by the Islam religion. Religion in our nation is fighting for its existence right now, not only against the liberal forces but against Islamic infiltration.

Religion has partially been alleged as the cause of some of the major unresolved conflicts around the world. The two most prominent examples are the conflict between India (Hindus) and Pakistan (Muslims) over the disputed territory of Kashmir and the Israeli-Palestinian (Jews-Muslims) conflict in the Middle East.

In America, our nation and our government is being infiltrated by people who follow a religion (Islam) that wants to destroy us. It can only get worse!

This is the Shariia system. It advocates the dream of an Islamist conquest of the West by infiltration from within and attack from without: by the word and the sword, the two-headed serpent. The future they envision has only one obstacle in its way: American Constitutional Democracy in all of its expressions – freedom of conscience, freedom of speech, freedom of religion, equality between men and women, equality between Muslims and non-Muslims, and Western notions of personal liberty. This is why neutralizing America – its foreign policy as well as its vibrant social and political culture – is their obsessive quest.

The Liberals have successfully incorporated their ideology into our country in the last 50 years by 90-95%, per Liberal pundits. The end game of the Liberal Movement is to achieve a Socialism utopia that no Socialist Movement has ever achieved in history or ever will. Socialism is a failed historical political ideology.

What Liberals do not realize is there is another end game beside theirs that is in process; world domination by the Islam Religion per Muslim Caliphate. Islam is taking advantage of our Liberal dominated Western Civilizations right now to infiltrate our societies thru open immigration policies, permissive multiculturalism, globalism and basic Liberal naivety. The Liberals will never get a chance to achieve that illusive utopia because unless some major changes happen, within a few decades, America could be Muslim dominated per Islam Jihad.

There will be no "Crusaders" from the Roman Catholic Church this time, although Christians around the world right now are major victims of genocide from the Islam Caliphate. The current Pope is sadly a Globalist Liberal whose world views are actually facilitating the Muslim Jihad.

The Islamic caliphate represents a real and present danger to the peace and unity of the current world. This religion has had a major influence on the deterioration of the world to this day, and it is vital to understand the underlying theology of Islam.

Muslims have been dreaming about a caliphate that can unite the entire Muslim world and rule with a strict Islamic code ever since the death of Muhammad in 632AD. There have been coups, countercoups, and civil wars because of disagreements over whether or not to install a caliphate.

The dream of a caliphate is what is responsible for the Shia/Sunni split. Several caliphates existed over time until 1924, when Mustafa Kamal Ataturk abolished the Ottoman Caliphate and established the secular Turkish Republic.

Al Qaeda, the Taliban and I.S.I.S. have clearly stated that re-establishing the caliphate is one of their primary objectives. Although these terror groups have taken a violent path to realizing their dream of a massive Islamic empire, there are many Islamic groups all across the world that use politics to gain influence, such as the Muslim Brotherhood, Tanzeem al Islami and Hizb ut Tahrir.

What exactly is a caliphate?

A caliphate is the Islamic form of government representing the political unity and leadership of the Muslim world. The head of state (caliph) has a position based on the notion of a successor to Muhammad's political authority. It is a dream that has never been realized by Muslims, and it hopefully never will be.

There will always be Muslims who dream about this empire. On the other hand, power-hungry leaders will seek to prevent any movement that could dissolve their nation-state. Therefore, Muslims are stuck in an eternal conflict between Islamists and nationalists.

What are the goals of this caliphate?

Besides uniting Muslims, the goal is to arrange a massive Muslim army and call for Jihad against infidel states for the expansion of the caliphate. Various caliphates have used this strategy to expand their states. The rapid Islamic expansion during the reign of the caliphs is nothing but staggering, and we are currently seeing it happen again. The ultimate goal of the caliphate is to bring every square inch of this planet under Islam and to convert , subdue or kill all remaining civilizations (infidels).

The reason is that millions of eager men are willing to join the fight against the infidels because they believe that Allah will reward them after they die. There has never been a shortage of military recruits in the Arab world, and there is no shortage of suicide bombers today.

So what does the future hold? A massive Islamic empire, where outspoken voices, homosexuals, females, and other "immoral" people are executed on a regular basis? A world where females are property and life on earth has little value? A fascist empire expanding itself bit by bit through demographic and political conquest, as we are seeing in the modern-day world? Will the West have to constantly defend itself from Islamic aggression?

If the world does not wake up to this threat, the future of world civilizations, especially western democratic civilizations, looks gloomy.

3. Female Power Movement

"A pattern has been emerging during the last generation that was pioneered by the United States: a growth in the power and confidence of women and an erosion in the confidence of men. The female power movement has been a disaster to the nuclear family and the male and female relationship, religious values and to the health of our democracy. The last two generations of children are growing up rudderless in terms of the requirements of being a good, educated citizen."[11]

This power shift was necessary; women did need a more equal role in society. The problem is not that it shouldn't have happened; the problem is that it has overcorrected itself. The pendulum has over-swung the equilibrium radically, and the feminist movement is keeping the momentum going. A reverse correction has long been required.

The women's movement is a very misleading term for it suggests all women are involved, which is a fraud. The feminist movement was never about supporting all women, just radical feminist women. It was not designed to create an equal relationship with men; it was designed to change society to make life more suitable for radical feminists.

Feminism has manipulated human nature; they know it is easy to get people to identify with victimhood. The standard feminism motto is "equal rights for

---

[11] Hambleton, Chris (2014). *America at the Crossroads* (Kindle Location 735).

women." The problem is that feminism is not about equal rights at all; feminism is about political power for the radical feminist.

"Women, as a group, are now working more and earning more, while men are working less and earning less. "Starting in 1978, women were graduating from colleges at a higher rate than men and the gap keeps increasing. Colleges now have more female students (up to 60%) than male, with a trending male decline projected to continue." [12]

Our culture is conforming more and more to the female shape. An effective power group called the radical feminists has renovated and redesigned the public dialogue. They "own" formal and informal communication, much in the same way Microsoft became the universal language of computers.

As a result, "mother" and "housewife" have become embarrassing answers to "What do you do?" Public and private life, intimacy, and emotions swirl around so-called male oppression, while a large part of life in the public and private sphere has changed dramatically for the female – for the better.

Today, it is more controversial for a woman to not be working than to be unmarried. Marriage rates have been falling dramatically in the last 50 years and are at historic lows. Now, both men and women are obligated to work outside the home. The negative effects on children and relationships are enormous. Divorce rates are rising, children are suffering, fathers have lost the love associated with the family unit, and the mother is more stressed because of the additional responsibilities of being a single mother.

---

[12] Kirst, M. (2013). *The College Puzzle*, Blog, Stanford University.

"There has also been a shift in the economic power of men and women. In the 90s, women earned 7.6% more than in 1979, while men earned 14% less. Women also earned 40% of the family incomes by the 90s. In the 90s, 1 in 3 wives earned more than the husband. In 1968 it was 1 in 18."[13]

The implications of this shift include an enormous amount of responsibility associated with love and money over the last generation, especially for women.

Simone de Beauvoir, an early radical feminist, once remarked that women should not have children because they would want to be with them too much, which in her opinion would interfere with desirable social change. This is a sad statement, as the undisputed power of females, fertility and nurturing, has always been acknowledged and admired. Fertility and nurturing has never been of value to radical feminists and per ideology programming, most females today.

Meanwhile, the male fades out of the picture. Each instance of a single mother implies a father not included in the family unit, as divorce usually leaves men financially broke and without their children. They become outlaws and are expected to pay child support for children they may not even see. This has disenfranchised men from their traditional family role and explains the conflict, in part, of female resentment toward and disillusionment with men. In the undeclared war between the sexes, women are winning, but at a high cost — men and women have to remain involved with one another.

---

[13] Eyer, D. (1996). *Mother Guilt*, New York, Times Books, p32.

There have been some feeble attempts at a "men's movement," but no effective national entities exist in the US that reflect the interests of men comparable to the National Organization for Women (NOW).

Meanwhile, well-schooled graduates of college women's studies programs are assimilating into the social, business, and political arena, and they are becoming power brokers and decision makers.

There's also trends called "political correctness" or "woke", which are blurring the lines between public and private lives, between personal emotions and their public evaluation. The personal has become the political, which destroys any real communication between the male and the female.

The once idealized appeal of mother, father, and children has declined in importance in our social structure. The traditional nuclear family and the male and female relationship are disappearing.

Modern feminism was a large, effective catalyst for these changes. Feminism is not the self-evident revelation of scientific truth as proclaimed. It is simply an effective instrument of public power. Feminist heroines emerged with new ideas to describe a new land populated by sexually liberated, economically industrious, and independent females who no longer needed males.

Today, women can have sex without fear of pregnancy because of the birth control pill, and they have babies when and with whom they want, even in a test tube, if desired. Men have slipped down the usefulness ladder, and a new family pattern has emerged: a woman, a child, and a bureaucrat. A new breadwinner has emerged in our society: the government.

The inequalities did not disappear for either sex; they just created a more complicated, stressful world.

A new landscape exists today for what is right, wrong, good, bad, correct, and not correct: single motherhood, gender choices and styles, infertility, contraception, government handouts, sexual harassment, homosexual assimilation, abortion, adoption, and contractual human breeder issues. These conflicts were unheard of 50 years ago.

No man or woman could have foreseen the swift collapse of the male. No one could have foreseen the new direction that men, women, and families are now taking. Men and women appear to be cast in a new play that has a plot and stage directions so confusing they are useless. Players, critics, and audience are uncertain as to what the play is about or how it is going to end. There are two reasons this play is probably going to end badly.

The first and most obvious reason involves Charles Darwin's evolutionary principles and the Industrial Revolution. The male was the hunter, gatherer, provider, and protector; the female was the child bearer and nurturer. That was the order of things in Charles Darwin's world. As the United States evolved into the Industrial Revolution, hunting and gathering was replaced with industry. This changed the world as much as any religion has, but at a cost. It has removed morality and human nature from our society. The social, moral, and economic decisions now being made are shallow in nature and reflect on the poor results of societal changes.

The second reason is that the changes we are dealing with involve the power of the feminist movement, which resulted in social, political, and legislative changes. Underlying these changes is an ideological insistence that boys and girls are similar and, therefore, all communities must have similar interests, laws, and opportunities for both genders.

But are men and women really the same? In the 1970s, it became accepted that women were not just men's equals, but the same as men. A few small plumbing differences, but that was it. If only we could strip away the culturally imposed stereotypes, said feminists, we'd be exactly alike. That will be the future, to throw out all those tired, worn-out sex roles that a patriarchal society thrust upon us.

We would stop saying "viva la difference!" because, supposedly, there are no differences. We would equip little girls with miniature tool belts, have boys play house with dolls, and put everyone in unisex outfits. The rush was on to reform men into the Alan Alda male. Any males who resisted got the glare and were considered Archie Bunkers. This made all our lives, mine included, very confusing.

The loss of female femininity was a major setback to the male and female relationship.

Mother Nature engineered men to desire females and to feel energetically charged around us. They say they can feel this charge just by just thinking about us! Nothing makes a man feel more masculine than being with a feminine woman who recognizes and acknowledges his manly qualities and gives him her nurturing, loving, soft energy. Her femininity brings extra vibrancy and life to his masculinity. But a woman who forsakes her femininity reduces her ability to energize a man, weakening the bonding force between them. Like a trellis without a vine, a man can feel his existence becoming barren, gray, and harsh without the nurturing presence

96

of a woman in his life. It's been observed time and time again that married men are happier and live longer than unmarried men. Feminine women are the icing on their cake, the cherry on their plain vanilla ice cream.[14]

Women have rightly fought for equal rights with men. Yet, were they so eager to declare victory that they settled for less by willingly trading in their true birthright, their femininity, in exchange for equality? If men get to exercise their rights to remain in their natural masculine energy, while women have to suppress their natural feminine energy, is that really equality? How can women compete with men who are already great at being masculine? Why put themselves at this unfair disadvantage? Women were told they could have it all, but after half a century, do they? How can they realistically have it all when their operating as "imitation men" and not from their natural feminine essence? That's not equality—it's being a slave to political correctness and feminism. Women should never have had to give up their femininity to gain equal rights to men.

Adult males today are adjusting as best they can. The main concern is young boys. They are considered "defective" compared to the basic nature of the "perfect female." Schools and colleges are a one-sided warzone, and young males are losing the battle. These "defective males" are earning lower grades, are winning fewer honors, are less likely to go to college, and if they do, are less likely to stay in college, except in party mode.

Generations after the feminist movement began, men and women are still at each other's throats and drifting even further apart. Despite determined efforts at

---

[14] Wonderly, Morgan, *Simply Feminine: Surprising Insights from Men* Crescendo Publishing LLC, Kindle location 141-157, Kindle Edition, 2017.

non-sexist child rearing, little boys are still a rowdy bunch, and little girls are still proper. I hope this never changes.

Science has shifted as well. The assumption 50 years ago was that biology did not matter that much, but there is now accumulated evidence that men and women are different at their cores. Changes in the lives of men and women have definitely evolved into a new reality in this last generation.

Current Feminism trends called "gender fluidity" and "gender equality" are destroying the lines between the male and female. A person is allowed to choose their gender, even children and usually male. This will be a complete disaster for society.

This can be confirmed by asking any current female athlete if she enjoys competing against biological male athletes.

The absolute truth is that feminism has been a disaster for the American female. It did not free women; it just bewildered them, especially on a biological level. It made the lives of the male and the female much more discouraging and stressful. Women today are caught between feminism and their basic biology. Their female biology tells them sex requires love, marriage is important, children are important, and men are needed. Meanwhile, feminism tells them to sleep around, make your career a priority, avoid marriage and children, and if you do get married, no problem, divorce is easy. Is it any wonder that modern women are angry, frustrated, confused, and unhappy? Feminism is one of the worst movements that has ever happened to our country.

Hopefully, the male and female can get back together. For years, we have been drifting further and further apart, at great cost to society. Men and women have lost respect for one another and struggle to communicate. Marriage and family life, the bedrock of society, are disintegrating. Children are not getting proper emotional support and love. Today's world is complicated and stressful, and there is strife between the sexes as a result. Unless we can successfully adapt to one another despite sociological changes, our species as we know it is in danger of becoming extinct.

My hope is that men and women awaken to what we are losing and what needs to be done. For the mutual benefit of both sexes, we should fight to keep what worked in the past while adapting to the changes that have happened in the last generation.

4. Black Power Movement

Early Black leaders (such as Martin Luther King and Frederick Douglas) emphasized the twin themes of equality and self-improvement for the Black community. They demanded that Whites respect the country's basic political principles, while demanding that Blacks, beginning with themselves, prove capable of satisfying its highest standards of self-governing action and achievement.

Whereas in the struggle for political rights King had asserted that Blacks had the primary responsibility for their own struggle, in the economic arena, he was convinced to place the primary responsibility for progress upon the government. For him and for the movement in general, this involved accepting the ideology of victimization that emerged and gradually became prevalent during the 1960s and still is. As the victims of centuries of oppression, Blacks could not be held responsible for their circumstances.

Sadly, due to this kind of thinking, the focus of the civil rights movement shifted away from efforts to organize, strengthen, and develop the resources of the Black community toward efforts to lobby the government for massive federal assistance.

> "The quest for equal legal and political rights gave way to the effort to establish and maintain a network of government-based programs that became a kind of 'welfare plantation,' increasing rather than eliminating Black under-achievement and dependency." [15]

---

[15] Keyes, Alan (1988). *Those Who Would Be Free, Where the Civil Rights Movement Went Wrong* (Kindle

The ideology of "victimization" has robbed a generation of young Blacks, particularly in the urban areas, of this critical understanding. It also robbed significant elements of the Black community of the moral wherewithal to defend against destructive internal and external forces. Victimization became the excuse for crime in Black neighborhoods and the collapse of personal moral discipline among the young. A generation taught to regard itself as the helpless pawn of historical and social forces learns nothing about the dignity inherent in personal moral responsibility – the dignity inherent in freedom.

> "Only when the Blacks return to this culture, the twin themes of equality and self-improvement for the Black community, will they find the means to save the portion of the Black community that is today receding into a long, dark night of permanent social and economic collapse." [16]

Another major issue for our democracy from the Black Power Movement is the disintegration of the American Black family and the associated family values from the dependence of Black people on "entitlements" or "reparations" at the government trough in a state of mind called "victimization." All of these issues destroy any chances for many Black children or adults to appreciate and enjoy the fruits of a real democracy.

Race and racism are also major issues in the United States of America. Undeniably, the concept of race is a primary component of the American narrative. It's a topic that's as old as the United States itself. It's an uncomfortable topic for many, but one that's impossible to escape. Not an hour goes by that there isn't an incident that has been deemed an example of racism from the liberals. These race-

---

p175–176).
¹⁶ Keyes, Alan (1988). *Those Who Would Be Free, Where the Civil Rights Movement Went Wrong* (Kindle p177–178).

related incidents usually get left bias publicized by the media, and controversy usually follows. The sad current trend involves liberal designated victims (75% of the country) creating a hoax claim against a conservative, then media running with it, with no fact checking or repercussions when wrong.

No one would deny that racism exists, but there is also general consensus that racism was once far more predominant than it is now. Despite racism's decreasing predominance, many believe that Black Americans still contend with serious, systemic racial discrimination on a daily basis. In fact, racism continues to be blamed for many of the Black community's troubles. As a result, many Black Americans view racism as their most formidable threat. But is racism really as prevalent and systemic as Black people presume? Or do most Black Americans simply blow the threat of racism out of proportion? The answers to those questions, respectively, are "no" and "yes." No, racism is not as prevalent and systemic as many Black people claim it is. Yes, most Black people blow the threat of racism out of proportion.

Many factors can influence a person's mental capabilities, but skin color is not one of them, and the majority of Americans know this. But if the majority of US citizens know this, why are Black Americans often seen as inferior? Why is it that Black people seem to be subjected to unequal, subordinated treatment in America? Black people are indeed treated poorly in America, but race and racism have just about nothing to do with it. People don't treat Black Americans as second-class citizens because of their skin color; they treat Black Americans as second-class citizens because of their culture. If a group of individuals willingly adopts senseless and destructive cultural standards, people will rightfully think less of them, and unfortunately, many Black Americans willingly embrace senseless and destructive cultural standards.

Not all Black Americans espouse negative cultural traits (the Makers), but the depraved behavior of millions of Black ghetto gangsters and entitlement queens (the Takers) has inspired other races to have contempt for Black Americans as a whole. No one is going to respect a person or a group of people who willfully endorse toxic and immoral cultural and behavioral lifestyles. It's just not going to happen, especially if that group of people behaves as if they don't even respect themselves. The perception that Black Americans are culturally and behaviorally degenerate is exactly what breeds dislike, disgust, and a lack of respect from other races. Therefore, when Black Americans are treated in a manner that seems unfair or prejudiced, it has more to do with behavior and culture than anything else.

"In other words, some Black people get treated as second-class citizens simply because many of them choose to act like second-class citizens. When a group of people is discriminated against because of their behavior and culture, the term culturism is far more befitting than racism. When Black Americans are discriminated against or treated like second-class citizens, culturism is almost always to blame, not racism."[17]

The actions of some affect the perceptions of many. The actions of some Black people have tarnished the image of Black America as a whole. As with the conditioning reflex associated with Pavlov's research, non-Black people have become subconsciously conditioned to associate negativity with Black skin. This negative association is based on the fact that, all too often, Black skin is connected with crime, brash behavior, or some bad statistic (such as rampant out-of-wedlock

---

[17] Hampton, Scott (2014). *Why African-Americans Must Stop Blaming Racism for Their Problems and Start Taking Responsibility* (Kindle Locations 321–248).

pregnancy rates or astonishingly high crime rates). This negativity is also reinforced by news media bias.

In America, culturism has taken racism's place, and the only things preventing Black people from prospering are the negative aspects of Black culture they allow to persist and flourish.

Sadly, most of the well-known negative stereotypes pertaining to some Black Americans are accurate reflections of how too many of them choose to live their lives.

"It's ironic that some Black Americans make such a huge issue about negative stereotypes while, simultaneously, doing everything they can to substantiate and enforce negative stereotypes. Negative stereotypes will always persist just as long as some people continue to behave in accordance with these stereotypes. In recent years, people in America have made it seem like stereotypes are a proxy for racism. But, in actuality, stereotyping is directly related to culturism. After all, stereotypes are derived from an analysis of a group's culture. Therefore, stereotyping (negative or positive) has almost nothing to do with skin color. It just so happens that some people with black or white skin choose to fulfill negative stereotypes."[18]

In school, history has been regarded as boring because it celebrated White conquest at the expense of people of color. Black youth do not take an interest in learning about human history because they hear about all of the supposed achievements of White people, while only learning about how they were slaves.

---

[18] Hampton, Scott (2014). *Why African-Americans Must Stop Blaming Racism for Their Problems and Start Taking Responsibility* (Kindle Locations 430–452).

I experienced a similar environment in my school years with my American Indian ancestry. All I ever learned in American history was that American Indians were savages who should be domesticated or eliminated.

Again, we can't rely on others to do for us when we should do for ourselves. History helps us to understand ourselves and others; it's important that we learn about ourselves and others and understand our place in the world and why the world is the way it is.

5. Indian Power Movement

The Native American in North America has had a long road to travel to be where they are today. These people spent 30,000 years evolving, produced hundreds of different tribes, were at an advanced hunter/farmer stage in their development, and had a North American population of approximately "10-25 million people" at their peak in North America.

The Europeans never did realize the distinctiveness of each tribe of Indians.

The most spectacular example of diversity is language. Linguists speculate that at the time of the European invasion in the early sixteenth century, some four hundred different languages were spoken in North America.

The European Conquest period started in the 1400s, and never really ended against the Native Americans until the late 1900s.

After the Europeans decided that America was not their desired trading partner, India, their focus changed. America became that vast unsettled New World that had immense financial and conquest potential, trade and land. Trade and land to Europeans were wealth, power, and freedom.

In another significant contrast, the Europeans arriving in these regions (the British, the French and Dutch) were primarily interested in settling; they wanted to develop the New World as their own home. Their interests directly clashed with the indigenous population. The Spanish were only interested in exploitation and trade.

Europeans determined rather fast that the Native American was not going to be their source of cheap labor. Native Americans, because of cultural reasons, especiallymales (free spirit, family structure, pride), would not adapt. This necessitated bringing in Black slaves from Africa. The downside of this situation for the Native American was that Europeans also had come to the conclusion that the Native American was disposable.

By the last decade of the nineteenth century, the total Native Indian population had declined to about 250,000 people (estimated at 10-25 million people in North America before the Europeans arrived). Over 1,600 wars, battles, and skirmishes, as well as a dozen deadly diseases (smallpox, influenza, measles, scarlet fever, tuberculosis, cholera, whooping cough, typhus, diphtheria, chicken pox, and typhoid), had sent the Indian population into a downward spiral. Such a rapid demise convinced some people that the American Indians would disappear from the face of the earth.

By the end of the nineteenth century, the Indian "threat" against America's frontier had been eliminated, mainly through violence. Defeated in war and confined to reservations, the Indian nations' population that had once filled the continent had been reduced by 98%.

The twentieth century has been an erratic era of challenges, problems, and major adjustments for tribal communities and their governments throughout the West. Public impressions viewed Indians as the vanishing race in the late nineteenth century, as second-class citizens in the early decades of the twentieth century, dangerous militants in the 1960s, and nonexistent for the remaining decades until Indian gaming reminded forgetful Americans that there are indeed Indians in the United States.

The Indian people in the United States have been rising from the ashes over the last few decades. The sovereign reservations are becoming very self-sufficient, financially and politically. Indian tribes contribute to the employment of Indians and non-Indians, invest in the infrastructure of surrounding communities, and help to revitalize depressed regional economies. They have also funded important language and cultural revitalization programs.

Cultural sovereignty is possible because, since the 1970s, Native Americans have expanded their exercise of tribal sovereignty, and they have gained a degree of economic autonomy. In the last quarter of the twentieth century, Indian people empowered themselves through political activism, gaming and economic development. We can see the result of these efforts in literature, the arts, popular culture, and education.

The Indian Nation is thriving; they are becoming a wealthy, highly taxed entity in our current society. They are successfully transitioning from socialist states (reservations) to capitalist states but there is the irony in their situation. They are escaping the socialist state environment on the reservations, but the United States is moving toward becoming a socialist country. The issue that the sovereign Indian Nations will face in the evolving United States socialist environment; sovereignty and capitalism are not compatible with socialism.

The Indian power movement did not have the negative effects on our Nation that the liberal, feminist and Black movements did.

American Indians are a vibrant part of twenty-first-century American life, not merely as individuals but as citizens of sovereign nations (reservations).

4. United States of America is at the Crossroads

There are many reasons for our present socioeconomic woes and the extent of America's demise. This book takes a look into what is occurring in America today and the path we seem to be heading down, which is similar to those of other great societies, like the Roman and the Greek civilizations, which, while once great, fell to their demise over time. While many may argue that America is not as great as we believe, America has been in existence for almost 250 years, which in and of itself is an accomplishment.

In 1887, Alexander Tyler, a Scottish history professor at the University of Edinburgh, had this to say about the fall of the Greek Republic some 2,000 years prior:

> "A democracy is always temporary in nature; it simply cannot exist as a permanent form of government. A democracy will continue to exist up until the time that voters discover that they can vote themselves generous gifts from the public treasury. From that moment on, the majority always votes for the candidates who promise the most benefits from the public treasury, with the result that every democracy will finally collapse over loose fiscal policy, (which is) always followed by a dictatorship."

Per Professor Tyler, the average age of the world's greatest civilizations, from the beginning of history, has been about 200 years. During those 200 years, these nations always progressed through the following sequence:

From bondage to spiritual faith;

From spiritual faith to great courage;

From courage to liberty;

From liberty to abundance;

From abundance to complacency;

From complacency to apathy;

From apathy to dependence;

From dependence back into bondage.

We are now somewhere between the "complacency" and "apathy" phases of Professor Tyler's definition of democracy, with some 50% of the nation's population already having reached the "governmental dependency" phase and increasing.

Unless some major changes happen in the direction of our Nation, the pending obituary of America is:

"United States of America, Born 1776, started dying in 2008"

America, while a leader in innovation and democracy, is sliding into a downward spiral toward demise. It may be a generation until this is totally complete, but surely, America remains on a downward curve and is heading towards "something else." Early America was all about discovery and frontier. Mid America was about production and automation. Current America is about equality and kindness. Future America looks bleak.

America was built on core values that were religious in nature. The core values outside of religion were born of capitalism. Work hard and get rewards.

Don't work and get nothing. This was the core of the country, and it is becoming diluted as we move forward. Capitalism, while it has its faults, remains the core reason America is as great as it was and still is. The reason it works is simple. If you have the ability to become rich with hard work and some luck, then you inspire others to try harder and innovate.

They say that other areas of the global economy are taking over where America can no longer compete. Labor is something that can be obtained more cheaply and efficiently in places like India and Latin America, but this is not the core of what America has to offer. In America, due largely to capitalism, we spawn the ability to innovate with new ideas, new products, and new technologies that set the stage for the rest of the world. It is this innovation that will continue to keep America strong and a dominant player in the world.

However, keeping those core beliefs strong around capitalism is a delicate balancing act, as there are those who now challenge it, people who believe socialism is a better way and capitalism is unfair and needs to be destroyed. If you take capitalism away from America, then indeed it is over, and the country will cease to be a dominant player in the world. We will once again move to a dark age when innovation is stifled and everyone does the minimum necessary to be equal and survive.

The current and future generations of America fail to understand this and allow the creation of false visions of world peace, equality for all, an end to world hunger, and love for all. The world doesn't work that way and never will. There will always be wars and people who will attempt to wield power over the free people of the planet, and if we are not careful, we will hand over our freedoms.

The first decades of the twenty-first century are leaving a mark on America that will hasten the end of the Republic. It began with the creation of something new in American life: a new generation that is disappointed, angry, educated, and connected. They could organize, protest, and disrupt the establishment far more effectively than previous generations of young people. By 2020, this "Lost Generation" will turn against the system in ever-increasing numbers. It has started to happen already in the 2016 elections with the Lost Generation's support for a radical socialist named Sanders.

The damage done in these first decades is not simply economic. It undermined America's faith in all leadership. Those years saw scandal and failure in business, finance, economics, government, and even religion. Business firms like Enron and MCI turned out to be frauds and empty shells. Giant banks and corporations like General Motors were bailed out using taxpayers' money, while millions of ordinary people lost everything. Governors of states like Illinois went to jail for fraud and corruption. Financial firms like Bear Stearns and Lehman Brothers, supposedly run by America's brightest minds, collapsed into bankruptcy dragging down innocent investors with them. Government bureaucrats, especially at the Federal Reserve, assured the world that they now had a perfect understanding of the economy, and there would be no more violent ups or downs in the business cycle. Religious leaders were shown to have covered up or even aided perversion in their churches. Sports heroes confessed to taking performance enhancing drugs. Who could you trust? The Republic was dying because its leaders in business, sports, politics, and even religion could no longer be trusted or believed.

During a single week in November of 2011, the American people learned that a "super committee" of Congress could not agree on a budget cutting plan after months of trying, that John Corzine, the former president of Goldman Sachs and former governor of New Jersey, had driven his investment firm and many of its shareholders into bankruptcy, that Merck & Company, once a paragon of corporate responsibility, had agreed to pay a fine of almost one billion dollars for criminal activity and, oh yes, Thanksgiving was that Thursday. Thank God, it was a short week!

Americans had always had a gentle, almost humorous skepticism about political leaders, but now that feeling hardened into total contempt. Politicians at all levels were regarded as incompetent, dishonest, or both. With good reason, young Americans began to think of their elders as fools who had squandered their future and burdened them with impossible debt. They looked at the previous generation and saw bankers who grew rich by wrecking the economy, politicians who resembled clowns, religious leaders who were corrupt, and educators who had failed them completely.

"The young people who came of age in those years will play a central role in destroying American democracy. Decades before, America's 'Greatest Generation' had been the children of hardship who became the parents of victory and greatness. The 'Lost Generation' were the children of privilege who became the parents of division and despair. Something very basic has changed in our Republic."[19]

---

[19] Gibbon, Edward (2013). *COLLAPSE: UNITED STATES HISTORY 2000 to 2050* (Kindle Locations 1133–1134).

Citizen Character and Morality

The integrity of all democratic and republican forms of government relies upon the personal character and morality of their people. When personal virtues and morals decline or even collapse, society strengthens the police and government in an attempt to keep the former degree of order. In the voting booths and then general society, the decline usually takes longer to become evident as people increasingly vote for more public benefits for themselves from the government's treasury. Soon political opportunists arise and take advantage of the faltering virtues in order to "save the society" – with themselves in control, of course. Within a matter of years or decades (depending on the form of government and the character of the people), the new society resembles very little of its former self.

> "The nation's character is being terribly wounded from within by abandonment of religious values, moral confusion, widespread immorality, lack of commitment, and negligence of our families, homes, churches, and schools. America is not only being torn apart by her own leaders, but by her own people: us."[20]

Social and political historians point to this lowering of standards as a primary cause of the violence and chaos that is bringing America to her knees.

Changes in cultural attitudes were reflected in the population. In 1960, out-of-wedlock births accounted for only 5% of total births; by 2005, this had grown to almost 40%. A huge body of statistics pointed to the fact that children born to single parents were far more likely to be raised in poverty, have educational difficulties, wind up in prison, or become drug dependent. Still, unregulated human

---

[20] Gibbon, Edward (2013). *COLLAPSE: UNITED STATES HISTORY 2000 to 2050* (Kindle Locations 574–578).

114

fertility is tolerated and even defended as a "human right." Few people would have disagreed that human reproduction should be regulated. All of this was well known to academics and government bureaucrats, yet they would not or could not do anything to stop it.

Where did that generation of Founding Fathers and the early American Republic get their virtues and moral standards from? How did America lose her moral standards, which had once been rock-solid? If modern America is lacking even most of its former basic values of civility, justice, and personal morality, is it possible for us to somehow renew those founding virtues and spread them throughout our faltering nation once again?

To the younger generation of Americans and far too many others, character and virtue fell by the wayside in the 1960s with the radical movement and the counter-culture. However, character and especially virtue in America were declining for most of the twentieth century thru the negative influence of progressive (liberal) ideology.

As a result of America's abandonment of moral standards, is it any wonder our families, churches, communities, and nation have broken down? Character builds nations, but immorality – and the disregard for moral standards of behavior – tears them down.

Instilling character and virtue back into the heart of our nation is far more important than our petty political squabbles, our education system, and even our economic problems.

Family and Marriage

The once idealized appeal of mother, father, and children has declined in importance in our social structure. The traditional nuclear family is disappearing.

Reality: men marry for beauty and females marry for money and security. Men and women have not changed their basic needs today, but women have changed where they get their money and security now.

Feminist politics have altered the public's ideas about male entitlement and instilled support for women in the economy, politics, and the courts. At a high cost to the traditional nuclear family, an additional family pattern called "bureaugamy" has emerged in the United States. This new trinity involves a woman, a child or children, and a bureaucrat.

Our generation struggles with a negative attitude toward marriage, and this affects how much effort we put into keeping a marriage successful. The greatest obstacle we face today is a lack of maturity and responsibility. Unlike previous generations, we are spoiled. Our culture of immediate gratification has not worked in our modern generation's favor. If everything is not just right, it's time to bail. Enter serial monogamy. Marriage requires work, but it can really be worth it.

Men and women used to have respect for each other before feminism came along. They knew gender differences were real, and each gender had its own strengths. Then feminism came along and told women they should be the same as men. Conflicts followed. The only way to restore mutual respect and communication between the sexes is for women to stop trying to be men. Respect your biology.

This does not mean men cannot share domestic duties and women cannot have working careers outside the home. Every relationship and every marriage is different. Find your balance, find your right mate.

Marriage is a desirable objective, and divorce should not be assumed to be an easy out. For centuries, marriage (pair-bonding) has been considered the foundation of society. Marriage provides a stable environment for children. Married people are more satisfied with their lives, happier in general, and make better and more productive citizens. In spite of feminist doctrine, most men and women want a mate to love and respect, and a family to protect and care for. Children need, deserve, and want to be raised by their own parents, especially in the early formative years.

The feminist movement has sadly undermined the value of motherhood and family.

We not only have a crisis in our government and public institutions, but we also have a threefold crisis throughout our society: exploding depravity, lawlessness and violence, millions of broken homes, and an absence of basic moral standards and even the values that produce them. The basis for every society, culture, and nation is the family, and the foundation of every family is the marriage.

> "The United States of America today has the highest divorce rate in the world (4.95 divorces per 1000, half of all marriages end in divorce) – is it any wonder our nation is in a shambles? If our homes are breaking apart and crumbling, then so follows our civilization. When our homes are divided, our nation becomes divided."[21]

117

Strong nations start with strong communities, strong communities start with strong families, and strong families start with strong marriages. If the heart of a nation could be examined, it would start with the families and the marriages.

The foundational unit of every nation is the family, and what is the state of the average family in America today? Broken, confused, angry, anxious, and distressed. Why are so many of our families broken and in shambles? Because so many of our marriages are broken, falling down, and being torn apart. As of 2011, America has the highest divorce rate in the world – even more than the secular, socialist states of Western Europe. Broken marriages produce broken families, which produce broken communities and then a broken nation, which is where we are today.

Another cause of the breakdown of marriages and homes in America is the "Great Society" welfare system started by LBJ in the 1960s, which has effectively replaced the father and his income with the federal government and the welfare check. The single greatest cause of poverty and violence in America, especially in the Black community, is the high absence rate of fathers and the lack of traditional homes. Good fathers provide stability and income to homes, but that interferes with the votes that are easily obtained from welfare recipients and others dependent on the government and the liberal politicians who thrive on it.

> "After all, the less that people are dependent on corrupt politicians (or any politician), the less likely they are to vote for them to stay in power. The welfare state (and now healthcare) is not about welfare or helping anyone — it's about wielding power over others, pure and simple."[22]

---

[21] Gibbon, Edward (2013). *COLLAPSE: UNITED STATES HISTORY 2000 to 2050* (Kindle Location 335).
[22] Gibbon, Edward (2013). *COLLAPSE: UNITED STATES HISTORY 2000 to 2050* (Kindle Locations 474–480).

Today, our own federal government is leading America down the same path that our Founding Fathers first rebelled against: tyranny from high taxes and infuriating regulations that resulted from vast, wasteful government overspending. But even those challenges could be overcome if our communities and families were as stable and strong as they once were. Marriages and families are the foundation of every society, and when they are strong, society is strong – but when they are weak, society crumbles and declines. Nations are only as strong and stable as their families, and America is no different. If America is to really recover and be restored, we not only need to get our fiscal house in order, but our homes and families in order as well.

Parenting

As a result of our faltering families and broken marriages, parenting in modern America has become more unpredictable and unstable than ever. Many parents today treat their children more like their little best friends than young people who need to be given guidance, direction, and discipline.

Because of divorce and the plethora of single-parent homes, parenting is often more difficult and stressful than ever before, because that one parent has to not only provide for the kids and maintain the home, but also play the role of both parents. One of the worst aspects of the modern family is the limited, neglected role the fathers have with their children, particularly in the case of divorce. Both mothers and fathers are needed, but fathers are critical in the development of character, virtue, discipline, and courage as the children mature.

Mothers are the most influential for character and virtue during the children's formative years, but fathers tend to be the biggest influence on kids as they enter adolescence and mature toward adulthood.

The female power movement has also been a disaster to the nuclear family and the male and female relationship and to the health of our democracy. The last two generations of children are growing up rudderless in terms of the requirements of being a good, educated citizen.

As parents, it is us and us alone who are responsible for instilling character, virtue, and values at a young age in our children and then continuing until they leave our homes. Are our careers more important than the character of our kids? Decent societies begin with decent homes and strong families; the goal of parenting is to produce moral, well-adjusted young adults.

And please don't confuse decent homes with meaning how fancy they may be. The exterior residence we call our homes isn't nearly as important as the family who dwells inside. In America today, we have far too many luxurious homes with bankrupt families inside, much like our brand-new school buildings that are full of students who can barely read and write at their grade-level.

Parents are to impart their values, heritage, and wisdom to their children – not solely the schools, the churches, or the communities. If we want to fix our country, we must invest in the next generation – the liberals and degenerates in our popular culture certainly are. It's time we took responsibility for the precious gifts who have been entrusted to our care. It is parents, not schools, peers, or pop-culture who should have the greatest influence in our children's lives.

Education and Learning

"If one needed proof that the United States was in trouble in the early 2000s, they need to have looked no further than the education system. In the year, 2000, the average fifteen year old American student placed twenty eighth on a standard math and science test administered worldwide. A Liberal endoctrination and control tool called Common Core was introduced in 2009 during Obamas presidency, the World rating dropped even lower."[23]

America was still home to the best universities and research establishments in the world, but also home to some very poor schools. In fact, there was no system of education in the America of 2000. Instead, there were hundreds of local school systems organized at the town, county, and state levels plus a collection of private schools. Obviously, this made for a very mixed set of results.

"The mean IQ of people living in the Western world has dropped about 18 points since the Victorian era. In the United States, the average IQ of its citizens is decreasing about 1.5 points each generation."[24]

An ignorant people will quickly become an enslaved people. Only an educated populace can be permanently free. What the educational institutions of a country teach, lays the foundation for either liberty or bondage. In recent years, where socialists have taken over countries, one of the first things they have done is assume control of the educational system. Education must not be government controlled; it must stay in the private sector. Even this will not totally solve the problem; the teaching environment and content in America's education system has been taken over by liberalism and feminism in the last 50 years. In America today,

---

[23] Merrill, Daniel C., M.D. (2014). *AMERICA IN DECLINE*, Xlibris US (Kindle locations 376–378).
[24] Merrill, Daniel C., M.D. (2014). *AMERICA IN DECLINE*, Xlibris US (Kindle locations 378-380).

even if a child is instilled with a wonderful set of values and morals by parents, he or she is totally reprogrammed to liberal ideology by the time they graduate from our educational system.

The federal government's top–down funding of American education is not working (for example, Baltimore) and never will, except to complete one of the requirements for a proper socialist state.

There was another consequence of this imbalance in American education. When the economy was growing at a good rate, the demand for workers was sufficient to absorb all of the university graduates even though they had no practical skills. As economic growth slowed or stopped, American business and industry could find little use for students of anthropology, political science or social justice warriors. A good many young people found themselves in possession of a useless degree and a very large debt from student loans. The default rate on these loans soared, currently 40% in 2016, and a generation of disappointed workers was created.

The experience embittered many members of the "Lost Generation," and they turned against the social and political system in large numbers. That unhappy generation is welcoming a drastic change in government – socialism – or as we know it today, liberalism. Sadly, they feel that they have no chance for success or happiness under capitalism. The irony is that liberalism has put them in this situation, not capitalism.

One of the primary pillars of secular philosophy and the liberal movement is the idea that with enough education, every problem in society can be solved. Utopia, that magical, wonderful place with no anger, violence, war, crime, or even unhappiness, is just a short distance away if we all have enough education and higher-learning.

The debilitating costs of college education are only part of the problem facing the younger generations.

"The biggest problem with our universities is that they purposely tear down the values of the students and indoctrinate them with secular, liberal thinking. Since the 1960s, most young people go off to college with the values instilled in them by their parents, churches, and communities and then emerge with an entirely different set of values. That's evidence of indoctrination or even brainwashing by our higher education system."[25]

So far, the results of alternative education have been very encouraging, particularly with home schooling or Charter Schools. Children are retaining their parents' values, achieving better results on standardized tests, and are actually allowed to enjoy their childhood while they can. If you can remove your children from public school and homeschool or Charter School them, consider doing so – odds are they'll have far fewer problems when they're older.

A child who becomes a good, educated citizen starts with a strong nuclear family unit that includes parents who love, care, and discipline.

Constitution and the Bill of Rights

A government of liberty is a government of laws, not of rulers or of the majority. In a pure democracy, a simple majority (just over 50%) of the people

---

[25] Hambleton, Chris (2014). *Restoring the Republic (Our American Awakening: Book 3)* (Kindle Location 1326).

rule, and the rights of the minority could be in jeopardy. Therefore, the best form of democracy is a constitutional democracy, in which the law is supreme and protects the rights of all people. A constitution defines and limits the power of government. It acts as a chain to bind rulers and keep them from misusing power. A constitution is written, so it will not be forgotten. Any government is free to the people under it, no matter what structure it has, when the laws rule and the people are a party to those laws. Any government opposed to this concept is one of tyranny. A constitution formed by the people should not deny the rights of others. The laws should apply to all people equally, regardless of political position, religion, race, wealth, social status, or creed. Everyone should be equal before the law in relation to protection of their life, liberty, and acquisition of property.

Under the Constitution as it was originally written, tyranny from one branch of the government is very difficult to achieve if the other branches are functioning properly. The Framers rightly understood that power always corrupts, so they fashioned the Constitution in such a way that the three branches would challenge and contend with each other. All three branches were to be equal in power and have the ability to prevent one branch from becoming tyrannical, and thereby threaten the natural rights of the American citizens. And for most of the last two centuries, the Constitution has protected America far better than any other form of government that rules over any other nation on Earth.

Sadly, the Constitution and the Bill of Rights are both under attack in our Republic by the Socialists. A society based upon the Rule of Law and self-governance can only function properly when morality and virtue are upheld by all. When personal virtues and moral standards crumble, so does the Rule of Law. Because of the degradation and laxity of our values and standards over the years, the carefully designed system of checks and balances in the Constitution and our Bill of Rights has been subverted by liberal political forces.

The Constitution, written in 1787, had worked well for more than two centuries. A crisis occurred in 1861 when 11 of the old state units tried to leave the Union in a dispute over slavery, but the Civil War settled that matter; nevertheless, imperfections remained.

Starting late in the twentieth century, the Constitution began to fail. Changes in society and political reality overtook it and it could not adjust quickly enough to survive. Like a dinosaur facing the reality of a new climate, it was doomed. Several problems troubled the Constitution. The relationships between Congress, the President, and the court system led to gridlock on a number of critical issues. Congress itself had internal problems it could not overcome, and the presidential election process was breaking down completely. The federal courts seemed willing and able to interfere in any area of private or public life, and activists of all types tried to use them to do just that.

> "I will argue that nothing, in this respect, will change significantly as long as the country is governed as a liberal socialist democracy, our direction since the 2008 election. Thus, to save America and its innate culture, constitutional conservatives will be forced to separate themselves from the liberal socialists, whose policies per the 'Entitlement Doctrine' are destroying the country's financial well-being and will leave her morally bankrupt."[26]

---

[26] Gibbon, Edward (2013). *COLLAPSE: UNITED STATES HISTORY 2000 to 2050* (Kindle Locations 474–480).

When the original Constitution was written in the 1700s, Thomas Jefferson had suggested that each generation of Americans should call a new Convention for changing the Constitution, but this has not been done for almost 250 years – long overdue. Constitutional conservatives need to develop popular support for an updated American "Constitution" per a national "Constitutional Convention."

Hopefully, an updated Constitution will restore the health and direction of our Democratic Constitutional Republic but if that is not to be, I welcome the opportunity to fight to the death for the God-given freedoms bequeathed to us by our forefathers.

Religion and Values

One of the great founders of the American religious system was the Rev. John Cotton (1584–1652), who made basic to colonial government the premise that Godly law and order means limited power and limited liberty. Neither man nor his civil governments have the moral right to unlimited power or to unlimited liberty. At all times, it must be power and liberty under law, and ultimately, under God.

But today we have demands for both unlimited power and unlimited liberty, which are mutually contradictory ideas. We also have the growing claim that liberty is not under law and under God, but outside the law. There are those who believe that they can only be free by denying the claims of all law, and by affirming that true rights and true liberty mean a freedom from law.

Americans, reared for some generations in the Biblical perspective, have seen freedom as life under God's law, but many today assert that freedom is escape from law. The alternatives to freedom under God, to liberty under law, were declared clearly by Karl Marx. They are twofold. First, one can have anarchism, every man a law unto himself, with no law, and total "freedom" from any responsibility to anyone. Second, one can substitute the state for God, and the total law of the state replaces the law of God. Freedom then disappears and total statism or communism for man's "welfare" takes its place.

This is a denial of liberty as a "bourgeois" ideal and a substitution of state-planned welfare for freedom as man's truer happiness. Every attempt, therefore, to remove this Republic from "under God" means that either anarchism or communism will surely result, whether planned or not by those who strike at God's place in American life. It is an inescapable alternative.

To restore true liberty, we must restore true law. The Bible speaks of "the perfect law of liberty" because it views God's law as the very source and ground of man's liberty. We must abandon the dangerous idea that freedom means an escape from law: this can only be true if the escape is from communism, which is not true law, but tyranny. The word tyranny is an ancient Greek word with a simple meaning: it means secular or human rule instead of law, instead of true freedom under God. The true American system is neither anarchy nor tyranny, but freedom under God.

Religion works best as a force of resistance, a conscience to society that keeps itself at arm's length from the state. The closer it gets, the less effectively it can challenge the surrounding culture and the more perilously it risks losing its central message.

When the church accepts as its main goal the reform of the broader culture, we risk obscuring the gospel of grace and becoming one more power broker.

With all the God-talk in politics today, younger voters may be surprised to learn that evangelicals' love affair with politics is a recent phenomenon. In the past, conservative churches did little "meddling" in politics, emphasizing instead personal behavior and preparation for the next life. They accepted their minority status in the world, and not until the 1980s did anyone start talking about a Moral Majority. Galvanized by social issues like abortion and gay rights, evangelicals got organized, attended caucuses, and ran for office. A clear pattern soon emerged, as demonstrated by many polls: the more prominently Christians entered the political arena, the more negatively they were viewed by the rest of society.

What happened to cause such a shift? An overwhelming majority of non-churchgoers associate these descriptors with Christianity: anti-homosexual, judgmental, hypocritical, old-fashioned, too involved in politics, not accepting of other faiths, confusing. As one interviewee expressed it, "Most people I meet assume that Christian means very conservative, entrenched in their thinking, anti-gay, antichoice, angry, violent, illogical, empire builders; they want to convert everyone, and they generally cannot live peacefully with anyone who doesn't believe what they believe.

Religion is under attack in our Republic. Life is often difficult and challenging, and it's easy to look at the world around us and feel helpless or even hopeless, especially when evil seems to be increasing. Everyone, but children especially, need regular doses of common-sense moral teaching. Our churches and synagogues used to provide these moral reinforcements, but with the rise of secularism, many people today derive their morals from whatever media and books they consume – most of which are secular or even anti-religious.

As a result of widespread secularism and declining numbers, too many churches either preach a watered-down, defective Gospel and semi-Biblical values, or they preach a feel-good social message that is relative only to the culture. A multitude of other churches have become apostate and no longer hold to Biblical standards or Scripture at all.

Although it often appears as a great monolith, religion is a diverse and multifaceted tradition that has evolved over the long course of history to adapt to the press of cultural and political change. In continuity with its past, the future of religion will have to incorporate new ideas into its theology, organizational structure, and everyday practices.

Current social issues must be addressed by religion to ensure the success of the church in the twenty-first century. Capitulation is not required, but recognition of the issues is very important.

The major areas of current concern is a globalist, liberal Pope, tightening priests moral standards, female priests, divorce, cohabitation, abortion, euthanasia, homosexuality, and biotechnology, which includes test tube births, sex selection, cloning, gene therapy, and stem cells.

America was founded to be a religious nation – though certainly not a theocracy – in which the Gospel could be freely proclaimed and people were able to worship as they saw fit. America was intended to be a land of religious liberty, in which no person's freedom of worship was restricted, provided they were not breaking the law. Throughout history, whenever religion and the government were joined, other religions or denominations would be persecuted. With such a wide variety of denominations and religions in America, the Framers of the Constitution made it neutral with respect to religion, so that no one denomination or religion could become the "established state religion."

The primary reason our country has been falling apart is because we are in a spiritual civil war with those who wish to tear our nation away from its religious moorings. The last major purging of our Judeo-Christian roots from our public institutions was the forced removal of the Ten Commandments from our courts and public schools in the 60s, the very places that Higher Authority must be cited in order to establish authority, recall our religious heritage, and maintain the Rule of Law.

Essentially, the Ten Commandments were America's moral standard, and people were simply expected to know and obey them. Much of early American law was built upon the Ten Commandments, and then more specific laws were added to address the various needs of particular people in particular areas. If our own courts and government have not only abandoned, but torn out the moral standard upon which American self-government was based, how can our form of self-government possibly continue?

For far too long, we have been apathetic in our duties to pass on our values, our heritage, and our history to the next generation and to those around us. We have been bullied and allowed our God-given rights to be trampled on by others who despise America and what she stands for. The time has come for us to stand up and declare, "NO MORE!" We are Americans and we are free — no one has the right to deny another's freedom of speech and religious expression. And though they may try, we must and will defend our rights.

Many Americans today are genuinely fearful about the demise of our country because of the unfathomable debt and the edicts emanating from our

130

elected officials. But even if we lost everything – all our wealth, our homes, our military, our freedoms – there would still be an America as long as it lives on in our hearts, minds, and souls. And as long as it continues to live on there, it will always exist.

The restoration of America will not come from the government, nor from Congress or the President — it can only come from us.

We built this country, but now it's falling apart. Let us set out to restore and revitalize it before it comes crashing down and is lost forever. We should try to always keep these four things before us: love of God, love of our families, love of our neighbors, and love of our country.

Heritage and Passing on Our History

One of the primary reasons the American Experiment has been failing over the last century is because of our negligence in passing down our American values, beliefs, history, religion, and heritage to the next generation.

When a nation forgets its heritage and history, it quickly loses its identity. This is one reason why liberals love to distort and rewrite history –because it causes people to question and doubt their heritage and heroes. Since the rise of liberalism, America's heroes and Founding Fathers have been marginalized, denigrated, and even vilified in our universities and, most recently, our public schools. Lately, very little room in our history books is given to them and their incredible accomplishments, in favor of providing additional room for the more recent history of the Liberal Era.

In addition to restoring our history curriculum, we also need to greatly increase the time spent on American history, and reduce the amount of time spent on the study of other nations that aren't nearly as important or relevant. How is it that many American students know more about Mexican history or African history than American history? A cursory study of African, Asian, and South American history is certainly useful for introducing students to those continents, but a study of American, European, and American state history should be taught over and over. If America is to continue as a nation, we must remember our history and teach it to the next generation!

This situation has been a major motivation for me to author the "Evolution Series" of books. The younger generation must be taught the real history of America and the world. They will be running this country in a couple of decades.

Biased and Negative Mass Media

Nothing can dampen one's spirit faster than turning on the news or picking up a newspaper or listening to a newscast these days. "Socialism is good, Capitalism is bad!" seems to have been the media's primary motto for decades. The media have discovered that the more horrific, violent, and biased the news is, the better it sells and the higher the ratings. When people have a strong emotional reaction to something, they become more likely to purchase or view it. But what does such repetition of violence and bad news do to peoples' attitudes and the society? A steady diet of terrible, depressing news soon creates the very society that once provoked it to outrage!

News media bias is real. It reduces the quality of journalism, and it fosters distrust among readers and viewers. This is bad for democracy.

Many prevailing biases exist in the US news media. All news outlets are biased toward a left leaning narrative. The Washington news media are biased toward Washington-based solutions. And the political press in the US has an overwhelming leftward tilt, mostly on social issues, but also on political and economic matters.

The leftwing bias of the American mass media is pervasive. Since the 1980s, studies have consistently shown that the professionals who constitute America's mainstream news media – reporters, editors, anchors, publishers, correspondents, bureau chiefs, and executives at the nation's major newspapers, magazines, and broadcast networks – are preponderantly left-oriented and the propaganda arm of the Democratic (Socialist) Party. Pravda on steroids!

Bias in the news media manifests itself most powerfully not in the form of outright, intentional lies, but is most often a function of what reporters choose not to tell their audience (i.e., the facts they purposely omit so as to avoid contradicting the political narrative they wish to advance). As media researchers, Tim Groseclose and Jeffrey Milyo, put it: "For every sin of commission . . . we believe that there are hundreds, and maybe thousands, of sins of omission – cases where a journalist chose facts or stories that only one side of the political spectrum is likely to mention."

By no means is such activity the result of an organized campaign or conspiracy. Media expert, Bernard Goldberg, says: "No, we don't sit around in dark corners and plan strategies on how we're going to slant the news. We don't have to. It comes naturally to most reporters." Goldberg explains that "a lot of news people got into journalism in the first place so they could change the world and make it a better place, and use their positions as platforms from which to show compassion, which makes us feel good about ourselves." Expanding further upon this point, Goldberg quotes researcher Robert Lichter of the nonpartisan Center for Media and Public Affairs, who said that journalists increasingly

"See themselves as society's designated saviors, striving to awaken the national conscience and force public action."

Or as ABC News anchor, Peter Jennings, admitted to the *Boston Globe* in July 2001:

"Those of us who went into journalism in the '50s or '60s, it was sort of the liberal thing to do: Save the world."

If there's one sector the liberals have a stranglehold on, it's the popular culture and the media. Most Republicans (moderates and conservatives alike) have yet to figure out how to effectively use the media to their advantage, rather than cowering in fear of it. The media is merely a mechanism, a tool that can be a powerful weapon when utilized properly and effectively.

Ronald Reagan was one of the few conservatives who could use the media to his advantage, often with good-natured humor but this would not work today.

To bypass the biased MSM and Hollywood, Trump was using social media, mainly email and Twitter. He was immediately lifetime blocked by Twitter after leaving office. Social media must be reigned in, section 230 must be changed.

The purpose of the media is (or at least used to be) to honestly inform the public of current events, and more space should be given to local and regional news, rather than national and global news. Opinion has very little relation to raw news most of the time, and the two should be kept entirely separate, which is the purpose of a news section in a paper or a newscast. Unbiased, objective reporting

134

is what most Americans expect from their news sources, but is usually not what they are given.

Biased Entertainment and Hollywood

Another significant cause of America's cultural decline comes from our national addiction to entertainment and Hollywood. Hollywood and the entertainment empires have taken it upon themselves to not only determine what American cultural standards are, but what they should be. When Hollywood was confined mostly to movies, it was relatively harmless; however, after the television was invented and Hollywood had a constant presence in our lives and homes, it soon began influencing our values and changing them into theirs.

It's becoming almost a cliche that whenever Hollywood celebrities campaign for some public issue, 98% of the time it's a liberal issue. Radical environmentalism, animal rights, abortion rights, anti-smoking, gun control, feminism, speaking out against a war, supporting Communist dictators or attacking sitting populist presidents are just some of the favorite past-times of liberal Hollywood celebrities.

So, if a bunch of Hollywood celebrities want to speak up for liberal causes, what's wrong with that? They have a right to adopt any cause they want, right?

Yes, they do have a right to adopt and speak out for any cause they want. But there are a couple of things wrong with this picture.

1. With a recent Gallup poll showing only 20% of the US population describing themselves as liberal and 40% describing themselves as conservative,

why is it that almost ALL of the political activism engaged in by celebrities is liberal in nature? Clearly, they as a group are not representative of the population.

2. Celebrities have tremendous access to mass communication channels and having their voice heard, yet most have little to no particular expertise, education, or experience in the areas in which they become "spokespersons." Recent info has shown that most have no more than a high school diploma, if that.

3. These liberal causes and attitudes do not just find their way into press releases and public appearances by celebrities, but into the very fabric of the shows, movies, and songs that are consumed by the unsuspecting American public.

4. The preponderance of liberal viewpoints being expressed by celebrities contributes to the misconception that liberal viewpoints are in the majority in America. They are not. They actually never have been.

The mainstream media in Hollywood and the entertainment industry are giving you a biased mix of information, often don't even present the conservative viewpoint; they are not doing their job. They're not representing the interests of the American people; they're representing a minority of the population and trying to convince us that their viewpoints are the way we must go.

The Abuse of Our Freedoms

Before the rise of the Feminist, Socialist or Black Power Era's, the abuses of our natural rights were relatively few and far between. The very idea that the majority culture had to change itself in order to accommodate a particular person's (or a minority's) wishes was unimaginable. If someone was offended by another's display of patriotism or religious expression, that was their problem. People had the common sense and understanding to realize that everyone at one time or another is offended by something, and that everyone is entitled to their expressions as long as it didn't damage another person or their property. Today, we've sacrificed much of our history, heritage, and individual rights on the altar of Socialism, Feminism and Black Power.

Our rich Judeo-Christian heritage has been all but stripped from our country, just because an activist group or even one person at times was offended. When someone from the ACLU becomes upset because of a graduation prayer or the simple sight of a Christmas tree or Nativity scene, the courts are quick to rule on the side of the one being offended, and that's if the offending group doesn't immediately surrender to the ACLU's demands.

However, the same judicial system that requires the removal of all religious symbols when one person is offended then turns around and adamantly protects the First Amendment rights of that person to then go and burn the American flag – the foremost symbol of the country that protects their rights to free speech and expression.

Feminism, Socialism and Black power tools must be eliminated: like political correctness, cancel culture, racism, multiculturism, police brutality, affirmative action, sexual harassment, victimhood mentality, gender fluidity, woke, me too, equity, etc.

As free people and citizens of the United States of America, we have every right to express ourselves the way that we see fit. When those who are offended threaten a lawsuit if we don't bow to their wishes, we should inform them of our First Amendment rights and then promptly ignore them. If they take us to court and the court rules against us, then we must appeal or even not comply with the court-ruling that violates our rights. A court of men has no right to violate our natural, God-given rights, especially when those rights are enumerated and protected by the Supreme Law of the Land: the Constitution and the Bill of Rights.

Multiculturalism:

Over the last several decades in America, it's become politically correct to refer to various groups and races of people within the country by prefacing their region of origin before "American"; i.e., "African-Americans" or "Muslim-Americans." Soon after the various races and groups in America were divided and categorized, the idea of globalism and multiculturalism set in, which tossed out the Great Melting Pot and replaced it with the notion that all immigrants could not only retain their own customs, languages, and lifestyles – but should retain them and not assimilate into America. Not only that, but globalism and multiculturalism and political correctness working together ends up forcing Americans to change to accommodate the various sub-groups, rather than those groups integrating into the existing American culture and adding their distinct culture/flavor to it.

In the United States, the issue of multiculturalism has been largely ignored. At the very least, it has either been inappropriately represented or misunderstood for years, perhaps both. As citizens, we have allowed ourselves to be convinced that diversity is a good thing for those within (and outside) our country. In some instances, encouraging diversity is a correct and appropriate position for the citizens of our country to adopt; in others, it is not.

Where multiculturalism causes a division within the country, it is detrimental. Division is created when a specific group refuses to speak the commonly accepted language and resists becoming part of the culture by refusing,

138

for example, to recognize the same holidays and demanding recognition of their own. These and similar practices cause community isolationism, narrowly define markets by cultural or geographic areas, or otherwise separate people into many distinct groups. This situation will be devastating to any country because it boldly stands as an obstacle in the way of developing or sustaining common goals and national bonds. Currently, Muslim (Sharia Law) integration, or lack of, into our society is such an obstacle.

Knowing a second language is one thing. Teaching our children the culture of our grandparents is a worthwhile endeavor. However, forcing one's culture (Sharia Law) on a section of our society and isolating that segment from the general population is quite another. It is absolutely necessary that we recognize the hazards that we bring upon ourselves when we allow multiculturalism to dominate our communities or overwhelm our nation, as Europe has discovered.

Do we want to live in a country where, when we travel from one community to another, we need to speak different languages, where some communities are likely to be resentful of "outsiders," where cultures do not mix, are not shared, and where people have nothing in common? Do we want to allow these policies to segregate our country and then wonder if it will literally come apart, as the Soviet Union and Europe has?

If the answer to these questions is no, then we must address the many issues caused by our present attitude towards these forces.

Abraham Lincoln said,

"A house divided against itself cannot stand."

Insofar as these forces divide our nation, our country is weakened. Today we see the insidious signs of globalism and multiculturalism everywhere. Unless we want a fractured and divided country where different languages are spoken, where anarchy reigns supreme, where people are pitted against anyone from a different segment of the population, where we cannot feel free or safe to come and go to other parts of the country or even to parts of our own towns, then we must recognize the dangers of multiculturalism and make the necessary changes. Either we do this, or we will continue down the path to more and more separate and individual societies, instead of building a single and solid, united American society.

Illegal Immigration and Santuary Cities

It is important to emphasize that the legal immigrants who reside in this country are not the problem. The vast majority of foreigners with green cards are productive members of society who work hard, play by the rules, and pay taxes.

Thru Obama and and Biden, nothing of significance had been done to curtail the flood of illegal aliens, including potential terrorists, who cross our Southern border on a daily basis because the Democrats see the newcomers as future members of their liberal voting bloc and big business, especially agribusiness, consider illegal's to be a cheap source of labor. Both of these self-serving reasons to skirt current law speak volumes with respect to our corrupt politicians and the self-serving people who support them. The open border and immigration loopholes created by the liberals are basically a long term strategy to build up their voting base.

"The criminal side of this unseemly narrative, 35% of all inmates in California's detention centers are illegal Mexican nationals, and nationwide, 29 % of those incarcerated in federal prisons are illegals from Mexico."[27]

The FBI also reports that half of all gang members in Los Angeles are illegal aliens from south of the Rio Grande. Rape, robbery, murder, and kidnapping are the norm rather than the exception for large segments of our illegal Mexican population as we read daily in newspapers throughout the Southwestern United States. Are you beginning to see the cost? Not only in monies but in human suffering, we are paying for allowing the Mexican underclass to set up shop in America. Clearly, our politicians have not!

"The criminality of illegals is only part of the problem. What about the economic drain they inflict on the country? Unfortunately, this part of the narrative gets worse, much worse! "Over two-thirds of all births in Los Angeles County are from illegal alien mothers on Medicaid."[28]

These births, of course, are a tremendous drain on the taxpayer. Worse yet, many, if not most, of the children born to illegals will become wards of the state. Unbelievable as it may seem, all children of illegals instantly become United States citizens the moment they take their first breath of American air. Insanity at its highest level, don't you think?

Throughout the country, our schools are inundated by cognitively challenged children who do not speak a word of English.

---

[27] Merrill, Daniel C., M.D. (2014). *AMERICA IN DECLINE*, Xlibris US (Kindle Location 534).
[28] Merrill, Daniel C., M.D. (2014). *AMERICA IN DECLINE*, Xlibris US (Kindle Location 535).

Our emergency rooms are flooded 24/7 with illegals requiring routine as well as emergency medical care.

> "Estimates on the costs spent on welfare payments to the families of illegal aliens range from 10 billion to 330 billion."[29]

I would argue that these items only scrape the surface with respect to the price we are paying for governmental policies that are allowing large segments of the country to be literally overrun by illegals from our Southern border and war refugees from the Middle East. Another reality: many of these war refugees from the Middle East are terrorists infiltrating America to do us harm.

> "Estimates on the number of illegal aliens in the US range from 11 million to 22 million."[30]

The Trump administration established proper border security and tightened up immigration procedures but the Biden Administration is going back to Obamas open border policies.

Strong, Independent Police Force and National Guard

Police and the National Guard power is a necessity in society to protect citizens from domestic enemies.

The police force is locally and regionally controlled and totally separate from military power. The heads of police forces should be elected and governed by local government. Police should be hired by the local government as employees.

---

[29] Merrill, Daniel C., M.D. (2014). *AMERICA IN DECLINE*, Xlibris US (Kindle Location 536).
[30] Merrill, Daniel C., M.D. (2014). *AMERICA IN DECLINE*, Xlibris US (Kindle Location 554).

The National Guard is state controlled and also totally separate from military power. They report to the governors of the states they are located in.

The death penalty should be automatic if you kill a policeman or National Guard soldier.

Private Citizens should be able to own their own weapons, thus giving everyone the ability to defend themselves from armies that have become pawns of the government. Protecting your property should be an inalienable right.

The current problem: Many of our nation's police forces and National Guards have been commandeered by state socialist bureaucrats; mayors and governors. They implement policies of selective enforcement, stand-downs, police defunding and are becoming pawns for their socialist masters.

Crime

We are paying a high price for diversity and an even higher price for not recognizing the fact that after 60-plus years of pumping money and a host of other social programs designed to lift the downtrodden minorities from poverty, the crime rate is many times higher now in minority communities than it was before Lyndon Baines Johnson began his infamous war on poverty.

The liberal press has refused to recognize the racial component of crime in the United States, and their failure to do so has contributed to the lawlessness that is so pervasive in our inner cities. For example, when reporting on inner-city crime, newscasters today seldom mention the race of the criminal because they believe it would be racist to do so.

There are several things we can do to decrease the crime rate in the United States. First, we must institute a National Identification Card (NIC) that will prevent illegals from entering the United States.

We must also concentrate our resources on crime prevention and spend less time and money on futile attempts at rehabilitation. Most attempts at rehabilitation for the adult criminal element should be considered for what they are — a total waste of time and the taxpayers' money.

To accomplish this goal, the punishment for crimes must be made so painful that the prospective criminal will think long and hard before he or she actually proceeds with a contemplated criminal act. We have been coddling criminals for the last 50 years, and guess what – it isn't working! We must return to the time when spending time in prison was a painful experience. Probation would be exceptional, and judicial practices such as parole, indeterminate sentencing, and judicial discretion would be eliminated entirely. Programs that attempt to rehabilitate the criminal element should be restricted to juveniles who are deemed not to have the mental capacity to understand the full gravity of the crimes they commit; otherwise, there should be a fixed sentence for every crime, and the prescribed sentences should be fully enforced, without exception.

In summary, we should do everything possible to reduce the criminal element in society by reconstituting the family unit, deporting criminal illegals, stopping illegals at the southern border and most importantly, providing jobs for all citizens who are willing and able to work.

Those who perform criminal acts should face swift and certain justice under laws that mandate fixed, inflexible prison terms for lesser crimes such as burglary, robbery, and mayhem, while those who commit murder should receive a speedy trial followed by a timely execution.

Healthcare System

President Obama made a critical mistake when he willingly turned over reform of the American healthcare system to Pelosi and Reid. Together, they concocted an impossibly complicated and expensive bill which ran for 1,017 pages. This is not a misprint; the law was actually over 1,000 pages in length and written in an alien form of bureaucratic gibberish. When it was voted on, literally no one, including the leaders of the House and Senate, really understood its effect. The whole process illustrated the systemic failure of government. Neither side in Congress seemed willing to listen to the other, while the President provided almost no leadership in this important matter.

Obamacare is failing to meet its promises of cost containment, affordability, and improved quality of care. It will never assure coverage for all Americans and is unsustainable in the long run. It has been flawed by political compromises and trade-offs from the beginning that favor corporate stakeholders in the medical-pharmaceutical complex over the needs of patients and their families.

Like it or not, we now have socialized medicine in this country, and we are only one small step away from a one-payer system similar to those of Canada, Great Britain, and all the other European socialized democracies. May God help us when, as is inevitable, we become seriously ill! One way or the other, the time is rapidly approaching when our fate will be determined by a death panel consisting of government bureaucrats and there will be precious little, or nothing, we can do about it.

145

Unfortunately, if we end up with a one-payer medical system, there will be nowhere for average Americans to go when they become ill; they will be stuck, as the average Canadian is now, with long waiting lines and, in the near future, death panels, whether they are rich or poor. Of course, as with most of the socialist policies that are being forced down our throats, exceptions will be carved out for our political leaders and the bureaucrats who work for them. Politicians and bureaucrats who are well connected will always have access to the best medical care available, at little or no cost, in medical centers like Walter Reed. That's the way it is and always will be in a socialistic society.

A major overhaul is required in the entrenched Medical and Pharmaceutical Industries to improve efficiencies and to lower costs plus pricing. This step would have to be completed before any kind of health care reform should be considered for our country; whether a single payer or a market-based healthcare system.

There is a non-political, more efficient, affordable, simpler and existing answer for our Nation's Health Care System.

Repeal and replace Obamacare with an updated existing system of proven value, Medicare for all "Paying Americans" – with full choice of physicians and hospitals, coupled with a private delivery system, costing most Americans and employers much less than they now pay. "Paying Americans" is defined as all citizens who are eligible by having paid or are paying into our National Social Security (Medicare) System per FICA withholding from wages.

Medicare for all eligible Americans and the VA would be handled on a National level with a private delivery system.

Incorporate all other government health care systems, including Medicaid and Chip, into the restructured non-political Medicare for efficiencies and cost savings only.

The delivery system and costs of all other government health systems, including Medicaid and Chip would be implemented and paid for at the state level, every state has different needs and priority levels.

Install must happen in planned phases to minimize the health care issues associated with Americans who must transition from Obamacare.

So what can be done to prevent the further erosion of our medical system? As with most of our social and economic problems, the answer is straightforward, but in our present political climate, it will not be easy to implement: we must totally repeal Obamacare and replace with the system described above.

Financial System

"It is incumbent on every generation to pay its own debts as it goes . . ."
– Thomas Jefferson

America was built on core values that were Protestant in nature. The core values outside of religion were born of capitalism. Work hard and get rewards. Don't work and get nothing. This was the core of the country, and it is becoming diluted as we move forward. Capitalism, while it has its faults, remains the core reason America is as great as it was and still is. The reason it works is simple. If you have the ability to become rich with hard work and some luck, then you inspire others to try harder and innovate. They say that other areas of the global economy are taking over where America can no longer compete. Labor is something that can be obtained more cheaply and efficiently in places like India and Latin America, but this is not the core of what America has to offer. In America, due largely to capitalism, we spawn the ability to innovate with new ideas, new products, and new technologies that set the stage for the rest of the world. It is this innovation that will continue to keep America strong and a dominant player in the world. However, keeping those core beliefs strong around capitalism is a delicate balancing act, as there are those who now challenge it, people who believe socialism is a better way and capitalism is unfair and needs to be destroyed. If you take capitalism away from America, then indeed it is over, and the country will cease to be a dominant player in the world. We will once again move to a dark age when innovation is stifled and everyone does the minimum necessary to be equal and survive.

How has it come to this? The simple answer is that the United States government has been spending (and promising to spend) trillions of dollars it does not have, and is enabled to do so by the nation's central bank: the Federal Reserve. At the core of our economic problems is the Federal Reserve, which encourages a debt-based economy rather than an asset-based economy, along with irresponsible government borrowing and spending. Like most central banks, the Federal Reserve is a perpetual debt machine, and will continue creating debt until it's either severely regulated or put out of existence. The Federal Reserve not only enables, but encourages our government to be wasteful and spend vast amounts of money it does not have. The Federal Reserve creates money out of nothing and floods our banks and economy with their banknotes, which has almost completely destroyed the value of the US dollar.

148

"The real value of the dollar has dropped more than 95% since the Fed was created in 1913. "The Federal Reserve has a nightmarish track record of incompetence and is largely responsible for causing both the Great Depression and the recent Great Recession by its monetary policies. If the Federal Reserve System had never been created, the US economy would be in far better shape and far more stable."[31]

At the end of World War II, the United States was the greatest industrial power in history, but by the 1970s, it was undergoing a process of "deindustrialization." Some of this was intentionally planned. Economic leaders moved manufacturing jobs overseas and planned to shift to a service economy. It was naive to think that an economy the size of America's could prosper by simply providing services. Many important innovations started in America but were then shipped overseas for manufacture. American industry should have concentrated on high-tech, high-end manufacturing as was the case in Germany, Switzerland, and Japan. Instead, capital flowed into industries such as financial services where huge profits could be reaped by small numbers of highly skilled people.

A manufacturing economy is far more efficient at distributing wealth than a service economy.

The temptation to make huge profits in finance, especially high risk finance, led to a series of scandals, frauds, and bailouts. This started with the savings and loan collapse in the late 1980s, and continued with the "dot com crash" in the 1990s and the "sub-prime mortgage" fiasco of the early 2000s. It will end with the generalized financial collapse in the 2020s.

---

[31] Hambleton, Chris (2014). *America Divided (Our American Awakening Book 1)* (Kindle Locations 416–423).

"The early years of the twenty-first century had seen numerous frauds, crashes and miscalculations that eventually led to widespread distrust of the financial system. As one mishap mounted on another, Americans began to suspect, rightly, that those at the top of the financial tree had fixed the game in their own favor. They witnessed as executives of banks and investment firms collected huge bonus payments while the investors, stock holders and the 'suckers' who had bought into these schemes paid the price. These people became wealthy not by producing goods or services that typical citizens understood and wanted; they profited by manipulating financial markets to their own advantage, often destroying the security of average people. There were very few prosecutions for these misdeeds because those guilty knew how to stay barely within the law while deceiving ordinary people or because they were too well connected to the government. In many cases, they were the government. Executives from top financial firms moved in a constant stream from Wall Street to key policy positions in Washington and then back again."[32]

Debt is closely related to America's economic decline and to the widespread social disorder of the twenty-first century. For now, let us say that of all the follies committed by current leaders, the accumulation of public debt is the most difficult to understand. It was as if they are intentionally steering the ship into a huge iceberg! How can they imagine that it will not sink? It comes down to simple stupidity, a fear to face facts, and the selfish desire to push the problem on to some future generation. By 2020, that future generation will be here and not happy about paying.

---

[32] Gibbon, Edward (2013). *COLLAPSE: UNITED STATES HISTORY 2000 to 2050* (Kindle Locations 1183–1185.

Young Americans are graduating from school only to discover that there is no American Dream waiting for them. They were born into a society that expected ever-increasing wealth, a GDP that would grow without limits, and an automatic pass to a successful career. Many of these young people have spent 16 years educating themselves to do nothing. They have no economically viable skills and industry has no use for them. It is not surprising that they are disillusioned and angry about the hand dealt them. Their parents lived it up and left them the bill! Now these parents are growing old, demanding ever-increasing social and medical care at an expense they cannot afford. The voting power of "senior citizens" and the craven desire of politicians to remain in office at any price made this system impossible to break. This "Lost Generation" would be the mature adults who willingly accept socialism. No society succeeds unless most of its citizens believe that it is fair and gives people a chance to succeed.

Fixing the debt would not have been rocket science, but it would have required a discipline that was nowhere to be found. At the end of 1999, the accumulated national debt of the United States stood at 5.6 trillion dollars. This was a disturbing figure, but there appeared to be reason for hope and optimism. The economic expansion of the 1990s had increased government revenues at all levels. The federal treasury actually ran a budget surplus in fiscal 1998 for the first time in almost 30 years. This was followed by surpluses in 1999 and 2000, the largest (and last) in history. Bill Clinton had proclaimed that the era of big government was over and some thought that the government was on its way to long-term responsibility. There were projections of paying off the national debt completely by 2015. Instead, the situation would grow impossibly, incredibly worse. Many economic historians believe that by 2015 the "debt bomb" had already doomed the Republic.

The tax system itself is a monument to stupidity; it is an incredible morass of rules, exceptions, exemptions, and deductions that make no sense at all. Normal people cannot calculate their own tax payments and must rely on professionals to do so. Believe it or not, in 2011, the tax code of the United States was over 60,000 pages long! The failure to reform or even simplify the tax code is yet another sign that the American political system is failing. The tax structure has created a considerable industry devoted to legal tax avoidance and has encouraged criminal activity that escapes taxation altogether. Even worse, it has led people to invest badly needed capital in useless projects simply for the tax benefits, not because they make economic sense.

Inevitably, the debt, the crazy tax system, and the lack of political leadership is destroying the American economy. All of this is happening when competition from foreign producers is hurting American workers anyway.

"In 2011 the acknowledged unemployment rate was 9.5% but if one counted all the workers who had given up looking or accepted part time jobs when they wanted otherwise, the real unemployment rate was more like 20%."[33]

The Trump Administration made significant positive changes in the areas of tax simplification, reduction and job creation but is being reversed by the Biden Administration.

---

[33] Gibbon, Edward (2013). *COLLAPSE: UNITED STATES HISTORY 2000 to 2050* (Kindle Locations 997–999).

Political System

No nation was more blessed than the United States at the time of its founding. Washington, Adams, Jefferson, Madison, and Monroe would have been political giants in any age. The fact that they served as the first five presidents was impossibly good luck, but by the end of the twentieth century, America's political luck had run out. American political life was not in decline, it was crashing. The political class – the United States never had an inherited ruling class in the same sense as less fortunate nations. But if there was no ruling class, there had always been a political class of professional politicians, bureaucrats, and hangers-on who collected around government.

"At the heart of America's political class were the two institutions most responsible for the death of American democracy: the Democrat and Republican Parties, the 'Evil Twins.' These two collections of powerful, thickheaded, self-serving, stupid individuals maintained almost total control of the political system and guided the Great Republic on its path to destruction."[34]

Both parties claimed to have some overriding philosophy, but no one could tell you what it was. In reality, both were loose-fitting collections of special interests that had little or no regard for the common good. Both were supported by a small group of financial criminals who were steering the American economy to disaster.

---

[34] Gibbon, Edward (2013). *COLLAPSE: UNITED STATES HISTORY 2000 to 2050* (Kindle Locations 1111–1114).

Republican candidates ran on platforms of "no compromise" while Democrats did the same. The result was vacillation and stalemate at a time when clear direction was needed. The political polarization of the day made both meaningful spending cuts and tax increases almost impossible. Democrats would not allow any reduction in entitlement spending, and Republicans would not permit any increase in tax revenue. The result was a calamity.

One might argue that this situation had always existed, but in the twenty-first century there were several new aspects. The size and power of the American government had grown far beyond the wildest thoughts of the Founding Fathers. For decades, government in America played a relatively minor role in the lives of most people. Consequently, the political class remained small. Starting with the Income Tax Amendment, the Federal Reserve, and the Social Security Act of the 1900s, this began to change. The federal government became a source of benefits, an aggressive tax collector, and the enforcer of thousands of laws. It was the wellspring of millions of regulations covering everything from the type of lightbulb you could use to the speed limit in rural Montana. As government involvement in all things grew, so did the political class. In fact, it grew completely out of control.

By 2000, there was not one person in America who was not directly affected in a large way by the government. Because the government was so large, powerful, and rich, it was inevitable that many people had a professional and often a self-serving interest in controlling or influencing it. We call this group the political class, which includes career politicians, both political parties, public sector unions, lobbyists, donors, and special interest groups or individuals.

Taken together, these decisions meant that a small group of very wealthy people could buy huge influence over government. Getting elected and staying in office cost money, a lot of money, and the donors had to be respected. Those donors had purchased public offices and the office holders. A small group of faceless individuals could now give as much money as they wanted to buy elections. From then on, the United States Congress and the Office of the President would be completely dominated by professional politicians who were bought and paid for by special interest groups. This system is destroying American democracy.

It is mandatory that a citizen politician who has not been bought and payed for by the political class will is elected. One candidate was chosen by the people (Donald J trump) and he served one term as president but ran into massive resistance from the Globalists, Socialists and the established political class; their power and financial structure was being challenged.

In the early twenty-first century, Americans began to put their benefits, their advantages, their medical insurance, or their government payments ahead of the national interests. Citizens said that they wanted real solutions from elected officials, but when it came to the programs that affected them, they were unwilling to sacrifice. Both Democrat and Republican politicians loved their office above all things, feared being defeated at the polls, and would not vote for needed sacrifice. The "Greatest Generation" had passed and America was now ruled by the "Entitled Generation." The end was clearly in sight, but few could see it.

Because getting and holding elective office had become so expensive, those who could give large sums to political candidates had vastly more influence than ordinary citizens. In turn, the government now had enormous power to regulate and control the economy for the benefit of special interests. Americans were willingly giving up control of their own government. Of course, this produced a corrupt political system. "Public servants" and the special interests they represented are beginning to strangle the Republic. Some state and local governments are so dishonest that they constitute a joke. At one point, the state of Illinois had four of its governors jailed for corruption in a 40-year period. One of these politicians actually tried to sell a vacant seat in the US Senate to the highest bidder.

> "The damage done by Bush and Obama, especially Obama, in the early 2000s was largely responsible for the probable fall of America. It divided and demoralized the nation as never before. It left us with a political system consisting of two uncompromising parties of blockheads. That system simply could not deal with serious problems. The economic mess and the deficit gave rise to America's angry 'Lost Generation' and it was those young people who gave up on democracy and trashed the Republic."[35]

No American, living or dead, has ever experienced such a prolonged period of failed leadership; the people grew quite cynical about government. Historians look back on the Bush-Obama era as a tragic failure of democratic government. When America needed prudent, mature, and pragmatic leadership it got two presidents who were blindly devoted to the ideology of the right or left. The political system was poisoned by outright hatred between Democrats and Republicans, while the majority of moderate Americans were trapped between two sets of self-serving political parties.

In the days of our Founding Fathers, men went to Washington, DC to serve their country. Today, with rare exception, the career politician goes to our nation's

---

[35] Merrill, Daniel C., M.D. (2014). *AMERICA IN DECLINE*, Xlibris US (Kindle Locations 691–693).

capital to make money. It's really as simple as that! Unfortunately, the corrupt political practices that make them rich are ruining the country.

"Liberalism will lead to Communism."[36]

Even if Barack Obama had not been elected President and another milder, more typical liberal or progressive was in his place, the results would still eventually end up the same. Under liberalism, the State always becomes nearly all-powerful and the citizens merely exist to further the State (and at the behest of the State); therefore, the State's power becomes almost unlimited while the people's rights are severely restricted. Under the Constitution and the American model of limited government, the exact opposite occurs: the State exists solely to protect the people and their natural rights and, therefore, its powers are clearly defined and limited, so as not to infringe upon the peoples' inherent rights and freedoms. While liberalism at first seems innocent enough, in the end it always evolves (or devolves) into other forms of Marxism, depending on the society or culture. Nazi Germany espoused socialism while hating the communism of the Soviets, even though both were quite similar in that they elevated the State far above the individual. All forms of Marxism are in direct opposition to the Constitutional Republic erected by our Founding Fathers.

The solution to political corruption is simple and straightforward. Only those who contribute to society should be allowed to vote. If we are to have any chance of righting our floundering ship of state, career politicians and special interest groups must go. Many of the evils of our corrupt political system are made possible because politicians can remain in public office indefinitely, and the longer

---

[36] Hambleton, Chris (2014). *America Divide (Our American Awakening Book 1)* (Kindle locations 1599–1608).

157

they stay in office, the more powerful and corrupt they become. Most of our present-day public officials spend their entire adult lives in a state capital or Washington, DC. They accomplish this goal by pandering to special interest groups while in office and joining special interest groups after leaving office. In the case of liberal office-holders, passing legislation that taxes the productive members of society and redistributes their wealth to the masses of people who do not work, works for them politically. This type of political bribery should be illegal, but under our present democracy, it is nothing more or less than business as usual.

Also, legislation to install term limits is an essential component of any plan to curtail the corruption in our state and federal governments. The political corruption in Washington, DC could be curtailed greatly if we limited the president, congressmen and senators to two four-year terms. Term limits such as these would not solve all our problems, but it would be a significant step in the right direction.

2020 was a pivotal year for our country with two scenarios after that election.

If a *Democrat (Socialist)* moves into the White House: Socialism back on track, deterioration of America, division of our citizens, financial collapse, a liberal Supreme Court, a Socialist State being formed and the facilitated infiltration of Islam is America's future.

The best chance America has of keeping our constitutional republic was if a *conservative popular citizen politician* who is not part of the political class gets into the White House: socialism would be put on the back burner, the political class would be dismantled, the economy and the national debt would be addressed,

158

national healthcare, education, religion, immigration, Muslim infiltration, class warfare, crime, energy, military, and America's global role could be revised.

This is not what has happened: a Socialist (Biden) was elected per a very suspect election process.

God help America.

Re-invent the Republican Party

It's time to change the existing political system; it doesn't work anymore. There is too much polarity between the two current American political parties, working together is impossible. Our congress is in gridlock.

Everything we are told about politics in America today – that there is no middle ground between left and right, blue and red, Black and White, us and them – is wrong.

There is a large group of American voters that have been formed by President Trump – even a majority – who make up a new American political populist bloc that is passionate, persuadable, and very real. This voting bloc could very well re-invent the Republican Party.

To vote out the Democratic Party (Socialist Party), they must unify and expand the Republican Party. Rhinos and establishment Republicans must be replaced with populists who support the Constitution; as written.

The most important issue facing our Nation right now: ELECTION INTEGRITY! We must take the country back in the 2022 Congressional Election and the 2024 Presidential Election or our Constitutional Republic falls!

The American political system has re-invented itself in the past. Now is the time to do it again.

Energy

Global energy independence, using both fossil and environmental sources, is a necessity in the modern world.

The United States is a world leader and the nations of the world look to the United States for leadership. American energy independence is about world leadership.

A few economists and advocates of global free trade have voiced a narrow view of energy independence, claiming that it will mean a retreat from global economic interdependence, a direction that would disrupt the global free market and lead America toward economic and political isolation. Their view is not true. The United States does not need zero foreign oil imports to be energy independent. There is no reason to end oil imports from Canada and Mexico. Energy independence is not about protectionism.

Energy independence does not mean closed borders or economic isolation. Energy independence can be achieved by producing abundant and affordable alternative transportation fuels through advanced technology that enables all countries to do the same. American energy independence has been achieved by our new president and will lead to global energy independence.

Developing alternative fuels on a scale large enough to free the global economy from dependence on oil as the world's primary source of energy will create a seismic shift in the economic foundation of the world.

American energy independence will create hundreds of billions of dollars in new wealth, resulting in new jobs and economic stimulus not seen since the World War II civilian workforce mobilized behind the war effort.

American energy independence will be achieved when all cars, trucks, and buses on US highways, boats, ships, and barges on US waterways, aircraft flying US airways, trains on US railways, and off-road recreational, construction, and farm vehicles are powered by transportation fuels from the USA.

Trump achieved energy independence during his administration, the nation will be going back to energy dependence under the Biden administration.

The globalists have more power when the US is energy dependent.

Military

A strong military is paramount to the freedom and stability of America and the world. From the time America's armed forces entered World War I in 1917 until today, the United States military has repeatedly meant the difference between civilization and barbarism. It is no exaggeration to say that a militarily strong America is the one indispensable prerequisite for a peaceful and prosperous world. The witness of history, as well as our own common sense, bear testament to the fact that when America's armed forces are powerful, focused, and feared, the globe is a better place.

An Obama presidency downsized US Army, stretched too thin to fight two wars simultaneously, was judged "weak" in an annual assessment of US military power according to the Heritage Foundation's 2016 Index of Military Strength.

The declining state of the overall readiness of the force, long warned by leaders from all military branches as reaching crisis levels, was a major factor in the poor scorecard, according to the Heritage Foundation.

The US does not have the right force to meet a two-major regional contingency requirement and is not ready to carry out its duties effectively, said the Foundation. The two-major contingency requirement refers to the ability to respond to two regional conflicts simultaneously. Consequently, the US risks seeing its interests increasingly challenged and the world order it has led since World War II undone.

Dakota Wood, senior editor of the Index, stated:

"Threats against American interests are stronger and more numerous than a year ago; key regions are more unstable, and our military capabilities have weakened further over the Obama presidency, these are very disturbing trends."

In the twentieth century, the major wars were fought on an industrial scale. The combatants on opposing sides possessed the same sets of conventional weapons – machine guns, artillery, tanks, ships, vehicles, and aircraft. In the opening decade of the twenty-first century, only America could quickly, and at low cost, destroy all those weapons possessed by any other country.

Yet, we did not win the battles, much less the wars, in Vietnam, Iraq, and Afghanistan. Why? Simple: the enemy adapted. He took off his uniform and used our morality and befuddlement to overcome our technological advantages. By hiding among the people, he was safe from our firepower. The enemy lived in the cities and villages, or hid across the border, coming together in small groups and choosing when and where to initiate contact against our patrols. Our troops wear armor and gear weighing about 90 pounds. They cannot run 100 meters without being exhausted. So when the enemy shoots, a patrol gets down and returns a vicious volume of aimed fire. Except you rarely see a target, because the enemy isn't stupid. He has selected a covered position before opening fire. Most firefights last less than 15 minutes, because once a gunship or aircraft comes overhead, the enemy is doomed. So he shoots and scoots. Thus, the war goes on and on, because the enemy will not commit suicide by massing or wearing uniforms.

In the twenty-first century, due to our vast wealth and technologies, we have not been sorely tested. Our beloved nation does not have a martial spirit, and perhaps does not need one. It does, however, need a strong military infused with a warrior spirit.

President Bush rashly overstepped in extending war to include nation-building. President Obama ideologically retreated by imposing restraints that encouraged our enemies. Congress proved irrelevant, lacking the cohesion to play its constitutional role in declaring for – or against – war.

America has been drifting. That should scare us all.

In summary, under Obama, our enemies did not fear us and our friends did not trust us.

President trump reversed this situation but Biden will return us there.

United Nations, World Health Organization and NATO

The US needs to establish some new rules for dealing with the world countries in the political and economic arenas. We should no longer be the world's policemen and should stop paying countries to be our allies or friends.

163

While I can understand the reasoning around the United Nations and that it is a collection of countries from around the globe that have come together with the intention of making the world a better place, in reality, the UN has been and continues to be in large part a complete failure, run by communist and socialist cronies who are only interested in the demise of America and our freedoms so they can capitalize on our losses.

In addition, if the UN continues to make demands that overshadow our Constitution, we should pull out of it altogether and tell them we will not reenter it until they move away from attempting to place restrictions on our rights under our Constitution, which is the foundation of our freedoms, whether or not they agree with those rights. The Constitution of the United States is the basis of America, and it is what we fought for during our independence from England and in every war that challenged America. It is the cornerstone of America and should not be open to any foreign interpretation or attempts to change or limit it in any way.

Many religions have the same general principle of helping one's neighbor, doing a good turn daily, and helping your fellow man. These are all commendable principles and important to the fabric of being a human. However, they need to be tempered around what is possible and what makes sense. America has been driven, largely by the media, into a feeling of extreme goodwill, which on the surface appears wonderful but is eroding the fabric of the American responsibility to be accountable for ensuring the country remains strong. America has always been the humanitarian country and leader in helping those in need. Our basic Protestant values follow this course of helping one another and others. However, there should be limits as this has impacted America's ability to function internally.

Support for NATO inside America also began to drop as Europe was seen as less and less important, and support for NATO by other members is nonexistent, especially financially.

After American troops had kept Europe safe for 50 years of cold war, after we had guarded the city of Berlin while it was completely surrounded, German politicians were saying that they did not want their soldiers to die in an American war.

We should also limit or stop our contributions to the United Nations, World Health Organization, climate change and countries who do not respect America or might even consider us an enemy.

Globalism is not the answer to a good world. Nations should take of their own citizens first.

Meanwhile, America seemed to be in perpetual conflict at a virtually perpetual expense. The actions in Iraq and Afghanistan took the lives of thousands of American soldiers and cost over $3.5 trillion. Looking back, we can hardly blame Europeans for not wanting to participate in this disaster, but it still caused resentment in America. A growing number of Americans began to think that, with friends like ours, we did not need enemies.

Global America

Public opinion reports on Americans' attitudes toward foreign policy sketch a picture of retrenchment, war-weariness, and skepticism toward global engagement, even as there is also a growing concern that the world is increasingly unstable and dangerous. Nothing about this picture is new or controversial. Some may worry about it more than others, but it is now commonly accepted that the US is downsizing its international role, and that the administration, Congress, and the general public are more absorbed with domestic concerns than with foreign challenges or threats.

Crises and retrenchment shaped our US foreign policy during the Obama presidency.

Many factors complicated America's efforts to determine its world role during the Obama presidency. Economic weakness at home, comprising sluggish growth, high unemployment, and growing debt, among other phenomena, limited the potential scope of America's engagement around the world.

Another factor is the potential for a vacuum in world order, because no country or coalition besides the United States is either able or willing to replace it as the principal guardian.

An exhausted United States and a network of US allies that are unprepared to provide for their own security can hardly provide a stable foundation for a new world order.

What's needed to achieve a new American global strategy is political will and a strategic vision to meet the three interrelated challenges of supporting freedom, defending the national security, and restoring our nation's economic health.

The first challenge – reaffirming the historic American commitment to freedom in the world – involves making it clear that we will do whatever we can to support people fighting for fundamental rights, although we must insist that they take financial responsibility for their own success or failure

Committing ourselves to preserving US leadership in the world is, therefore, the second major challenge for US policy. This is not an expression of American arrogance or a reckless form of overreaching. The urgent challenge now is for the US to exercise leadership in a convincing manner so that the vacuum is not filled by hostile powers or by chaos and violence.

However, continued US leadership is simply not possible unless we address a third critical challenge, which is to bring the spiraling US public debt under control. Over the last decade, the gross federal debt has more than tripled to over $20 trillion and now exceeds the total national GDP. The gross federal debt is projected to reach $38 trillion by 2024 under the socialist Biden administration. This will bankrupt the US; which is the socialist goal, ask Argentina or Venezuela how this turned out!

While there are many reasons for the continuing surge in public debt, including the 2008 fiscal crisis and the wars in Iraq and Afghanistan, the principal factor has been socialist spending and Covid costs. Unless we can summon the political will and bipartisan consensus to reverse our domestic decline, no amount of strategic vision will enable the United States to exercise the kind of leadership that the world so desperately needs.

The Trump presidency was very successful in overcoming all of these challenges during his term until Covid entered the picture just before the 2020 elections, very suspect timing.

The United States may not be able to develop a grand strategy; indeed, in a world of ever-increasing complexity, perhaps the mere desire to attain one is unrealistic. What is certain, however, is that US foreign policy will grow more incoherent the longer it postpones a candid discussion on its role in the world.

The socialist crisis-driven foreign policy was inevitably going to succumb to disorientation and exhaustion. The United States needs to have a serious discussion about its role in the world – one that matches objectives and means.

The US needs to establish some new rules for dealing with the World countries in the political and economic areas. We should not be the World's policeman any longer and should stop paying countries to be our allies or friends.

Globalism is not the answer to a good world. Nations should take of their own citizens first.

The challenge we face today is as great as any in American history. Our national security and the values we cherish, in addition to the future of democracy in the world, rest on our ability to rise to this occasion.

5. Future of the United States of America

Today in America, we face a crisis, but one which has been slowly constructed by the hands of our own public trustees – and our own negligence – over the last century: exploding public debt, vast government regulations and bureaucracy, plus the trampling of the Rule of Law by our officials in the highest offices of the land. And while those challenges are daunting, there is really no reason why they cannot be overcome. America has faced and defeated similar challenges before – she only needs the will and the vision.

Since the early 1960s, something has dramatically changed in the deepest levels of American society. After the brief period of Pax Americana in the 1950s, it seemed as if some invisible switch was flipped in the heart of the United States, and the very fabric of the nation began quickly unraveling. Almost overnight, we went from light to darkness, from optimism to pessimism, and from America the Great to America the Guilty.

> "There are five pillars in every society that are responsible for preserving and passing along its history and values: the families, the religious institutions, the media (in various forms), the educational system, and the government. Some societies blend one or more of these pillars together while others separate and isolate them."[37]

---

[37] Hambleton, Chris (2014). *America Divided (Our American Awakening Book 1)* (Kindle Locations 217–221).

169

In the ancient world, the government, educational system, and religious institutions were often combined into some form of state-religion structure. Modern societies typically separate these pillars so they function independently, though over the last century, many societies have been steadily returning to the state-religion model under the banner of secular humanism (socialism).

The teaching of history plays a vital role in communicating, validating, and reinforcing a society's values. If a nation's values are directly attacked, the societal pillars and values themselves are often sufficient to repel the frontal assault and the foreign ideas are rejected. However, if the history of a society is gradually corrupted in a continuous series of small, indirect revisions, people begin to question where they came from, and soon they will start questioning and even rebelling against the society's long-held values and eventually accept the foreign values.

> "For much of the last century, but in particular the last fifty years, the history and faith of America's Founding Fathers have been under constant attack from secular revisionists, who are committed to replacing our traditional Judeo-Christian values of America with the values that more closely match their own: secular humanism."[38]

When a nation forgets – or is purposefully made to forget – their own history and heritage, they will soon forget their traditions and values. Eventually, the nation becomes unglued and unanchored and can be twisted and turned by whatever cultural or political winds are blowing.

---

[38] Hambleton, Chris (2014). *America Divided (Our American Awakening, Book 1)* (Kindle Locations 2953–2955).

Now you know how it is so easy for news reporters to do street interviews with random Americans, asking, "What US president is Washington, DC named after?" and most people do not know. Liberal indoctrination has been very successful in the last 50 plus years.

In American society, the education system (especially the public schools), the media, our churches, and our families are responsible for teaching America's history, about our Founders, and their rich heritage of faith and character that guided them. But sometime in the last century, the ties that bound those societal pillars together came undone, and suddenly they went their separate ways. The families stopped teaching their children and left that up to the schools; they stopped passing on their faith and values and left that up to the churches; and soon, the children began hearing contradictory messages between their families, the schools, the churches, and the media.

Today, the five pillars that were once bound together so tightly to keep America strong and united have completely broken down. Good families are few and far between, the churches are confused, weak, and behave more like social clubs than religious institutions. The educational system and media not only refuse to accurately teach about our history and our forefathers; they often teach the exact opposite, painting Washington, Jefferson, and Madison as wealthy, White (and therefore racist), slave-owning hypocrites.

If we are to heal our nation and restore America's national soul, we must first rediscover who we are as Americans. Because of a century of progressive revisionism, we cannot rely upon the media or our schools to accurately tell us, which means we need to relearn our history and our traits for ourselves.

On June 17, 1963, America's highest court in the nation – the Supreme Court of the United States – declared that America was now independent of God. In the case of "Abington School District v. Schempp," the use of the Bible in public school was ruled unconstitutional by the Court appointed by FDR, the Hugo Black Court. As Chief Justice, Hugo Black popularized the notion of "Separation of Church and State," used so often today in ruling against any (and all) religious influence in the country.

The First Amendment clearly states: "Congress shall make no law respecting an establishment of religion, or prohibiting the free exercise thereof . . ." Contrary to modern revisionism, the Founders weren't attempting to extinguish religion, as much as prevent a state-preferred religion from dominating the nation, as was commonplace in England and throughout much of Europe. The Founders were protecting the freedom to worship as everyone saw fit, and not destroy religion or even isolate it from the public square.

In fact, religion plays a critical role in every government and society, as it's the primary means of establishing and communicating the moral values of a society, especially to young children when growing up.

At the start of the twentieth century, one-half of the world's population identified itself with one of the five major religious traditions: Judaism, Christianity, Islam, Buddhism, and Hinduism. After 100 years of rampant secularism and scientific progress, that number now stands at nearly two-thirds.

Since the dawn of man, "community" has been defined almost exclusively in terms of proximity. In other words, "my community" is comprised solely of those who speak "my language," who live in "my community," who share "my faith," who are, in effect, territorially bounded together with me. But the Internet and mass communication technologies have completely upended how communities are created and defined.

Globalization has changed the very definition of community. Globalism is not the answer to a good world. Nations should take of their own citizens first.

"The pillars of our society which once held us together are not only crumbling and falling apart, but are systematically being torn down by the very people who should be upholding them, like our elected officials, teachers, lawyers, the media, and other cultural leaders. Our public servants have turned themselves into our masters, and there seems to be little recourse or accountability on their behalf. Tragically, America appears to be following in the footsteps of all the once-great nations and empires like Rome, and Greece."[39]

Those in the capital now seem to be acting as if they control the entire country and care only about how it affects them and not us. That's certainly not how most Americans think it should be. Will the entire nation go down with our capital? That appears doubtful; a significant portion of Americans today recognize the source of most of our problems: Washington, DC.

After two centuries of entrenched institutions, departments, and bureaucracy with few reforms, too much power has been accumulated in too many hands in the federal government, and people are sick of it (according to many of the polls). The various departments of the federal government have sufficiently insulated themselves from much accountability because the money always seems to be there. And with more and more sweeping edicts emanating from Washington, the capital

---

[39] Hambleton, Chris (2014). *America Divided (Our American Awakening: Book 1)* (Kindle Locations 2953–2955.

is becoming a stench in the nostrils of millions of Americans. The days of most Americans wanting bigger and better government are ending, but our two existing political parties, the lobbyists, the special interest groups, the public sector unions, the mainstream media, and the entrenched bureaucrats haven't gotten that message through their heads yet.

After the financial crisis of 2008, Americans have scaled back their spending, but the federal government has exploded their spending when they should be scaling back as well. The first rule of deficits is like the first rule of holes: stop digging! In the government's case, it's to stop spending. Americans used to revile communism and socialism, but now we have all but embraced it under the label of liberalism – to our demise.

After the financial crisis of 2008, Americans have scaled back their spending, but the federal government exploded their spending when they should be scaling back as well. The first rule of deficits is like the first rule of holes: stop digging! Or, in the government's case, stop spending.

The End of the American Dream - Overview in 2021

According to the Congressional Budget Office, the future Biden one-term deficit will total a forecasted $8 trillion, including the $1.9 trillion, spiraling to $11 trillion if Democrats follow through on next month's planned $3 trillion bill for "infrastructure."

Republicans have widely noted the huge waste in the current spending bill. Of $1.9 trillion, only $465 billion is due to the $1,400 check, putting the bill's pork and payoffs at $1.4 trillion. Economists have identified the enormity of planned spending, and its recklessness. Even stalwart Democrat supporters recognize the Biden administration utter disregard of fiscal responsibility.

It took 220 years for the USA to reach a 10 trillion dollar deficit. It took 20 years for Bush and Obama to add 10 trillion dollars to the deficit. Trump added 3.5 trillion dollars. Covid added 3.5 trillion dollars during his term. It is projected that Biden will have added 11 trillion to the deficit during his term. The total deficit in 2024 will be a projected 38 trillion dollars. This will put us well on our way to destroying the Constitutional Republic, which is the plan of the Radical Socialists. This plan worked for Hitler.

To put this into a personal perspective; every man, women and child in the USA in 2020 would owe over $50,000 to pay off this debt. This amount, by extrapolation, goes to $75,000 per person in 2024 per the current Socialist Biden budget projections.

To put this into a China personal perspective; every man, women and child in the China in 2020 would owe over $5,000 to pay off this debt in 2020. Not expected to increase by 2024.

The biggest victims will be the middle class and the "Lost Generation"; the well indoctrinated younger generation who has been taught that Capitalism put them where they are. Massive income redistribution is in our future that they believe will produce a wonderful Socialist utopia. Wrong – the majority of this transfer will go to the minority Socialist elites. The lost generation is cutting their own throats right now as far as their future.

The Democrats' spending program is a grievous assault on this nation's future, more serious and ultimately more dangerous than any crisis we have faced in the past. Wars can be won. Unfunded spending on this scale is surrender.

But that is not the full measure of the worst. Driving the country exponentially into ever greater indebtedness fairly and objectively marks the end of the American dream.

Socialists plan on destroying our Constitutional Republic and totally rebuilding as an autocratic Socialist State.

Please let this all sink in![40]

If America is to be saved, we must reject Socialism and Islam, return to our founding principles, and purge all trace of these ideologies from America. If we do not change course in both our culture and our fiscal policies immediately, our collapse will be painful, spectacular, and far worse than any before or any after us. If the collapse is imminent, how do we prepare?

As the collapse draws closer, we must organize by families, churches, and neighborhoods and become self-sufficient again. We cannot just stock up on food and essentials and expect to weather the storm by ourselves. If we don't quickly organize, the evils that occur in the midst of such chaos will only explode, especially if the crisis becomes desperate. We must be alert and understand that when the Rule of Law collapses, the police will not be able to protect us. Looters, rapists, murderers, and other criminals must be quickly and severely brought to

---

[40] Levin, William, *American Thinker* 03-19-2021
https://www.americanthinker.com/articles/2021/03/19_trillion_in_spending_11_trillion_in_oneterm_deficits.html

justice, rather than be allowed to run rampant while we wait for the police (who will be too busy to respond). This is yet another reason why "We the People" must all stay adequately armed and prepared.

"As long as there are those of us who love our country and bitterly cling to our American heritage (along with our Bibles and guns), there will always be hope for our country. When our Founders declared their independence from Great Britain, they knew they had a righteous cause — and so do we in defending and restoring our country. They were enormously outgunned and outnumbered, but they fought anyway because they knew it was the right thing to do. I believe that same spirit still lives in America, and it is growing. The vast majority of people in the country don't want a new form of government, they simply want the bad judgement and corruption expelled from the system. Most Americans want politicians who will tell them the truth — no matter how terrible and depressing it may be."[41]

In the context of history, America's current cultural war could be thought of as other great battles our country has had for freedom — America's struggled against socialism from Germany and Russia, and it now threatens to engulf us once again, with its throne firmly set in Washington, DC.

The time has come for Americans to decide whether the United States becomes a full-fledged socialist democracy (like the ones that are imploding in Europe), or returns to being a Constitutional Republic based on a Constitution, limited government and a strong religious foundation, managed by common-sense citizen statesmen rather than professional politicians.

---

[41] Hambleton, Chris (2014). *Restoring the Republic (Our American Awakening: Book 3)* (Kindle Location 122.

6. Conclusions

During his high-flying presidential campaign of 2008, Barack Obama declared that he was going to "fundamentally transform America." As typical at the time, the crowds cheered wildly and some even fainted at his carefully chosen words and manufactured charisma. However, what did he really mean by that statement? Isn't America her citizens – We the People – us and our fellow Americans? Would his supporters have cheered (and fainted) as they did if he would've promised to "fundamentally transform Americans" – the people rather than the abstract nation? And after almost eight years of his presidency, has he succeeded in his goals?

In the traditional measure of presidential success, Obama has been an utter failure. But he never said he wanted to become the best president – he said he wanted to fundamentally transform the nation. With that standard in mind, he has been an incredible success. He has kept very few of his campaign promises, often methodically, deliberately going against his own speeches, promises, and platform. Rather than have one of the most transparent presidencies, his has been rife with misdirection, corruption, division, and crony capitalism. That's another sign of a declining Republic: the election (and re-election) of willful, lesser men and women to high office who keep few of their promises and fill the government with corruption. But throughout his presidency, Obama has been consistent in that one broad, over-arching goal: to fundamentally transform America – and that means fundamentally transforming Americans. And he has been doing just that.

"Today in America, poverty has increased over 15% since Obama took office, the national-debt for the entire nation's history has risen an astounding 50% in four years, college tuition and health insurance costs have risen 25%, America's credit-rating has slipped from AAA to AA, the

178

average family's net-worth has dropped 39%, and the number of long-term unemployed has doubled to over 5.4 million people. The Misery Index has increased by 65% and the number of food-stamp recipients has risen nearly 50%. Like it or not, this was Obama's America."[42]

After eight long years, Americans were growing accustomed to being miserable, paying high prices for food, and energy, taking government subsidies/welfare benefits without a second thought, and not working or being productive. Indeed, Obama was fundamentally transforming America – by fundamentally transforming Americans.

And while he blamed his predecessor, George W. Bush, for the dire economic problems America was facing, his own policies greatly magnified them – just like FDR's policies during the Great Depression. Obama was changing Americans into the very people he and his wife regularly insult and denigrate: fat, lazy, over-indulgent consumers. But shallow, unaware, dependent voters are what he wants more of because they always vote for his party and other progressives. After 20 plus years of multiculturalism run amuck, people have either forgotten – or are forgetting – what it means to be an American. Our pathetic public education system, left biased and politically correct media, nanny-state governments, and twisted/perverted Hollywood entertainment industry have tragically altered Americans' self-image. We are becoming the very caricatures the mainstream media portrays us to be. Appallingly, Barack Obama, as the President of the United States of America, frequently echoed those same remarks, saying that America was

---

[42] Hambleton, Chris (2014). *America Divided (Our American Awakening: Book 1)* (Kindle Locations 2932–2939).

179

just as special as every other nation is, meaning that American exceptionalism is all in our heads. And of course, when everyone is special, no one is.

Not only that, Obama remarked several times that America is not an exceptional nation. If he thinks that, then why did he even bother running for the Senate or the Presidency? Who wants to help run a country they don't love with every fiber of their being? Perhaps one who means to harm or "fundamentally transform" that nation by holding a powerful leadership position. Most progressives may say they love America, but their reasons behind that affection are different than most traditional Americans. Progressives love America for her radical individualism and what they think could be another socialist utopia attempt.

The same patterns of behavior often appear and reappear in human events. Time and time again, economic ruin has preceded political and social upheaval, and this pattern is being repeated in the twenty-first century America. A number of factors combined to produce the "Lost Generation" of Americans who would give up on democracy and trash the Republic. None was more important than the loss of faith in the "American Dream" and the search for a replacement.

"'The American Dream' had been a compelling idea not only in the United States but also around the world. Our nation was called a shining city on the hill, a beacon, and the last, best hope for mankind. Many Americans also believed in 'American Exceptionalism,' the notion that their country was different from all others in history. This idea seems to inspire highly successful people, organizations and nations."[43]

---

[43] Gibbon, Edward (2013). *COLLAPSE: UNITED STATES HISTORY 2000 to 2050* (Kindle location 1145–1152).

180

Perhaps Romans once believed in Roman exceptionalism; they were certain that their empire could not go the way of Athens, Carthage, or Sparta.

At the outset of the twenty-first century, we are all faced with a bewildering array of challenges that 50 years ago we could never have imagined. On the one hand, the pace of technological change has confirmed humanity's cleverness; on the other hand, the persistence of global poverty remains a challenge to our sense of justice. We are increasingly interdependent globally and business opportunities abound, but rich and poor are as far apart as ever. We are addressed as consumers rather than as citizens in a materialistic society of great sophistication but with little sense of purpose.

The threat of nuclear war has not receded, and we are having to come to terms with the rise of global terrorism, the advent of the suicide bomber, and the resurgence of violence that is religiously inspired.

The breakdown of the family, particularly in the West, has laid heavy burdens on single parents, has threatened the cohesion of the community, and in many cases, has led to a sense of alienation.

We are confused about the nature of human identity, and this confusion can be seen both in the destruction of life through abortion and euthanasia and in our intention to create life through genetics and cloning.

Americanism can be summed up by what Dennis Prager refers to as the "American Trinity": Individual Liberty, Belief in God, and "e pluribus unum" ("Out of Many, One"). These three fundamental concepts define both the nation and the idea of America, and undergird her very foundations and institutions. If any of those three American fundamentals fall, the other two are greatly weakened and Americanism falters. The three fundamentals check and balance each other, yet also support one another. But at the center of the American Trinity is the belief in God, by which the other two cannot exist — the very "leg" that the progressives and the secularists have been attacking for the last century.

Those who set out to overthrow a country always start by attacking its history and foundations, followed by corrupting the civil institutions such as the universities, courts, and government that rest on those foundations. Then they step back and let the weakened nation collapse under its own weight of corruption. The secularists attacked religion first, then they attacked the integrity of the Founding Fathers, then they infiltrated the universities, the media, the seminaries, and then the various branches of government. After decades of their influence, America – by way of her corrupted institutions – is on the verge of collapse. The three centuries of stable foundations that began with our Founders have been thoroughly corrupted in the last several decades largely by the heavy influences of the Socialists and progressives (modern liberals or the Democratic Party).

Just as her people are living, breathing organisms, so America is a living, breathing entity – all countries are. All nations have a period of youth where energy, idealism, courage, and spirit abounds and they grow, sometimes to greatness and sometimes not. All nations go through periods of increase and decrease, rise and decline. Over the course of history, many nations and empires have even died violent deaths by foreign powers, while others simply grow old and feeble, and eventually pass away with the quiet gasp of abandonment like a ghost town.

Today, much of the West is not only in decline, but is dying. The "Evil Twins" of secularism and liberalism (socialism) have robbed the Western nations of their dignity, heritage, values, religious foundation, and history. The rise of the

European Union has done more to divide and denigrate the West than unite it; much of the West today is like a cancer-ridden, aging old man.

Hastening the death of the West is not only the fall of Christianity but also the rise of Islam, which opposes all things related to Western Civilization, especially America.

With the looming failure of the EU, nationalism is on the rise, but so much of their history and heritage has been lost that the people have no idea of how to protect their way of life, much less restore their countries.

The Liberals have successfully incorporated their ideology into our Nation in the last 50 years by 90-95%, per liberal pundits. The end game of the Liberal Movement is to achieve a naive utopia thru Socialism that no Socialist Movement has ever achieved in history or ever will. Socialism is a failed historical political ideology.

What the naive Liberals do not realize is there is another end game beside theirs that is in process; world domination by the Islam Religion per Muslim Caliphate. Islam is taking advantage of our Liberal dominated Western Civilizations right now to infiltrate our societies thru open immigration policies, generous welfare programs, permissive multiculturalism, politically correct ideology and basic Liberal naivety. The Liberals will never get a chance to achieve that illusive utopia because unless some major changes happen, within a few decades, America could be Muslim dominated per Islam Jihad.

There will be no "Crusaders" from the Roman Catholic Church this time, although Christians around the world right now are major victims of genocide from the Islam Caliphate. The current Pope is sadly a globalist liberal whose world views are actually facilitating the Muslim Jihad.

183

Where America differs from most other nations in the West (and the rest of the world) is that our times of decrease have been typically viewed as temporary setbacks and, therefore, have been brief. The Great Depression was an exception to this general attitude, when prolonged economic misery had dampened our outlook to the point that even our national spirit was filled with malaise.

Something deep within our nation is sick, or possibly even dying. We Americans used to be proud of our nation most of the time, despite her mistakes – and every nation makes them. Now that seems to be the exception rather than the rule. Now we feel brief, fleeting episodes of pride in our nation around the holidays, or when we see or hear stories of our soldiers and their bravery. But the general feeling of pride in whom we are as a people and what America stands for is gone, and no one seems to know how to get it back. At times, it seems as if half the country doesn't even want it back; that portion of the country seems to just want to take all they can get from the rest of us while they can get it, never mind that the country is being ripped apart.

In times of uncertainty and especially distress, people look to their government for stability and leadership. And while our elected officials provided solid leadership in the past, that no longer seems to hold true today. Like our country, our politicians are deeply divided as to their visions for the nation. Many of our leaders in Washington not only refuse to do anything about our problems, but exacerbate the divisions and tensions in the country for their own personal political and economic gain.

It used to be that we all had about the same picture for America, but we differed in our ideas of how to get there. Now, we have completely different pictures of what we want America to be, with roughly a third of us wanting to stay the course and maintain our heritage of liberty and limited government, while the other third is demanding equality on every level and cradle-to-grave socialist programs (such as in Europe), with the last third being undecided or even apathetic.

The foundation for a constitutional republic (as in the United States of America) can be described as follows:

"This form of democracy can only come forth and be maintained by a people that have the proper power or spirit within them. Without this foundation, a free government can never be established or maintained. It is not enough for a nation to copy some external form of government to secure liberty. That external form must flow out of the principles of liberty within the heart of the people. The pathway to liberty within a nation is from the internal to the external."[44]

From the hearts and minds of its citizens to the government.

"At the rate we're going, if America does not change course within the next five to ten years, she too will die and become like all the other great nations in history — merely history."[45]

In the coming years, we will find out if our Nation will be a Constitutional Republic, a Socialist State or a Nation fighting its second Civil War.

Our Nation does not want another Civil War but we also do not want to lose our Constitutional Republic.

---

[44] Beliles, Mark and McDowell, Stephen (2011). *In Search of Democracy* (Kindle Locations 131–137).
[45] Hambleton, Chris (2014). *Barack Obama vs The Founders (The American Tyrant: Book 2)* (Kindle Locations 2624–2626.

Per the 2016 election our Nation was given a reprieve to reverse the Socialist Movement by electing a Conservative Populist President with a mandate in Congress.

Socialism has had 50 plus years to establish itself in our Nation. The fight would be difficult but hope sprung eternal.

The Trump Presidency reinforced the reality that taking our Nation back from the Socialist Democrats is going to be a long, very difficult process. That Trump was able to accomplish as much as he did during his term was a monumental achievement (promises made, promises kept) considering how he was impeded every minute of his four years by the Socialist "Resistance" (Socialists, Democratic Party, Rhinos and many establishment Republicans, Left Stream Media, Hollywood, special interest groups and unions, high tech companies and social media, government imbedded socialists, the court system, etc.).

The Constitution, the Bill of Rights and the Ten Commandments were all trampled on by the Socialist Democrats.

Trump was trying to maintain the integrity of our Constitutional Republic during his term. His accomplishments during his "America First" doctrine were monumental. There was not a single area of our Nation that he did not have positive influence on, including protecting the American "Constitution".

A list of Trumps major Presidency accomplishments can be found in the Notes at the back of this book. An amazing list considering that I only placed his MAJOR accomplishments on this list.

As you might imagine, this situation was a problem to the Socialists! Trump interfered with replacing the "Constitution" with a Socialist totalitarian

186

government. The Socialist "Resistance" persecuted and tried to impeach him three times during his term and then removed him from continuing his second term with a suspect election. The American election process has been totally corrupted by the Socialists.

Biden became president in 2020 in a very suspect election. He is a moderate socialist but his agenda is being controlled by radical socialists including Obama handlers with Islamic influence. He is deleting as many of the Trump accomplishments as he can and is projected to be on his way to increasing the Nations deficit during his term by 11 trillion dollars – like Obama, another 50% increase in the Nation's deficit.

The future does not look good for our Constitutional Republic.

The End of the American Dream is approaching.

The coming decades will be a battle against Socialism and Islam to keep our Constitutional Republic.

God help us!

Today in America, we are facing big problems as a result of our negligence over the last 50 plus years. Few people love to study politics, much less war. Being involved in politics is often exhausting, frustrating, and depressing. Sometimes merely expressing your opinion in such a politically charged climate can cost you friends, relationships, or even your job. But if that's what is required at this time in American history, then let us rise to the occasion and meet the challenges and fight the battles head-on — if not for us, then for our children.

Do we love our children and grandchildren enough to say what our Founders once did, that if trouble must come, then let it happen in our day that they might have better lives? Do we love our country and our heritage enough to suffer for it, enough to make those tough, uncomfortable, painful decisions? Are we willing to be like our early American Founders and lay down our lives as stepping-stones across a raging river, so that our children may safely cross over onto the other side into the Promised Land?

Those are the decisions that turn ordinary men and women into founding fathers and founding mothers. Self-sacrifice and courage are what transform ordinary Americans into American heroes.

What I see is a great nation, an exceptional nation, by any standard, that has done more good for the world in more ways than any nation in history. It was able to do this because its brilliant Founders envisioned a system of government that allowed for the creation of an exceptional people. What bothers me is that so many people, including far too many Americans themselves, take for granted what America has meant and done for the world.

The reality is that America is not just any other nation. There is no country in the world that is willing to step in and play the benevolent role that America has. If America turns inwards and ceases to be the nation it has been, it will be a much darker world.

As faith in our American Dream dies, so will our Constitutional Republic.

Websites and Organizations

Please support these websites and organizations.

This list does not constitute endorsements of these sites: "I report, you discern."

Heritage.org – The Heritage Foundation, 214 Massachusetts Ave NE, Washington, DC 20002-4999

MRC.org – Media Research Center, 1900 Campus Commons Drive, Suite 600, Reston, VA 20191

GOP.com – Republican National Committee, 310 First Street SE, Washington, DC 20003

Democrats.org – Democratic National Committee, 430 South Capitol Street Southeast, Washington, DC 20003

NFRM.com – National Federation of Republican Women, 124 N. Alfred Street, Alexandria, VA 22314

RenewAmerica.com – Renew America Processing Center, P.O. Box 50502, Provo, UT 84605-0502

AEI.org – American Enterprise Institute, 1150 17th Street, N.W. Washington, DC 20036

Bibliography

1. Clark, Charles N. (2012). *Liberalism: A Subversive Force*, Kindle Edition.

2. *World Population, an analysis of vital data* (1968). Chicago, University of Chicago Press.

3. Hartman, David (2012). *The Downfall of America*, Kindle Edition.

4. Nies, Judith (2012). *Native American History*, Random House Publishing, New York.

5. Lewis, Jon E. (2012). *The Mammoth Book of How it Happened – America*, Kindle Edition.

6. Gibbon, Edward (2013). *COLLAPSE: UNITED STATES HISTORY 2000 to 2050*, Kindle Edition.

7. Merrill, Daniel C., M.D. (2014). *AMERICA IN DECLINE*, Xlibris US. Kindle Edition.

8. Hambleton, Chris (2014). *America at the Crossroads*, Kindle Edition.

9. Kirst, M (May 28, 2013). *The College Puzzle*, a Blog, Stanford University.

10. Eyer, D (1996) *Mother Guilt*, New York, Times Books.

11. Hampton, Scott (2014). *Why African-Americans Must Stop Blaming Racism for Their Problems and Start Taking Responsibility*, Kindle Edition.

12. Hambleton, Chris (2014). *America Divided (Our American Awakening Book 1),* Kindle Edition.

13. Rothman, Stanley (1998). *Roots of Radicalism Revisited,* Kindle Edition.

14. Clark, Will, (2015). *Islamic Two-headed Beast*, Kindle Edition.

15. Liberphile, A. J. (2015). *How to Defeat the Islamic State: A Holistic Punk Analysis of Creative, Politically Incorrect Solutions to the World's Worst Nightmare of Tyranny and Terror*, Kindle Edition.

16. Jackson, Brenda and McDonald, Ronald L. (1996). *Through Indian Eyes*, New York, Readers Digest.

17. Perdue, Theda and Green, Michael D. (2010). *North American Indians,* New York, Oxford University Press.

18. Fixico, Donald L. (2013). *Indian Resilience and Rebuilding*, Arizona, University of Arizona Press.

19. Keyes, Alan (1988) *Those Who Would Be Free, Where the Civil Rights Movement Went Wrong,* Kindle Edition.

20. Beliles, Mark and McDowell, Stephen (2011). *In Search of Democracy* Kindle Edition.

21. Hambleton, Chris (2014). *Restoring the Republic (Our American Awakening: Book 3)* Kindle Edition.

22. The World Bank Data (2016). *Fertility rate, total (births per woman).*

23. Hambleton, Chris (2014). *Barack Obama vs The Founders (The American Tyrant: Book 2)* Kindle Edition.

24. Wonderly, Morgan, (2017). *Simply Feminine: Surprising Insights from Men* Crescendo Publishing LLC, Kindle location 141-157, Kindle Edition.

25. Levin, William*, (03-19-2021) American Thinker* https://www.americanthinker.com/articles/2021/03/19_trillion_in_spending_11_trillion_in_oneterm_deficits.html

Notes

Note 1:

In-depth information on the subjects covered in this book can be obtained through other books I have written: the "Evolution Series".

This Series includes history that has been revised or removed from our National Education System to facilitate Liberal Socialist indoctrination:

The Evolution of the Modern Male and Female

The Evolution of the American Liberal

The Evolution of the Modern American Black

The Evolution of the Modern American Indian

The Evolution of the Christian Religion in America

The Evolution of the Islamic Religion

The Evolution of the American Democracy

The Evolution of the United States of America

Saving America

Available at Amazon and other retail outlets or on my book blog - EBook and Paperback - https://rcccabo.wixsite.com/richardcastagner

Note 2:

2016 – 2020: Trumps major Presidency accomplishments:

Reversing the ascent of the Islamic extremist terrorist group ISIS. Under his leadership ISIS has lost most of their territory and has been largely dismantled.

ISIS leader Abu Bakr Al-Baghdadi was killed.

Rebuilt the U.S. Military and reformed the VA.

Operation Warp Speed: accelerated development of coronavirus vaccines.

Moved the U.S. embassy in Israel to the capital of Jerusalem and re-supported Israel as a strong ally.

The southern border was made safe again per immigration reform and more than 450 miles of new and replacement border wall was built.

Led U.S. to a level of total energy independence (exporting more oil than importing for the first time in 70 years), allowing international policy decisions to be made with less regard to how an oil nation we once relied on would respond. Under Trump's leadership, in 2018 the U.S. surpassed Russia and Saudi Arabia to become the world's largest producer of crude oil. The U.S. is a net natural gas exporter for the first time since 1957.

The total number of Trump judges to be confirmed by the United States Senate is 234, including three associate justices of the Supreme Court of the United States, 54 judges for the United States courts of appeals, 174 judges for the United States district courts, and three judges for the United States Court of International Trade.

Drastic reduction in regulations, opening the door for entrepreneurs and businesses to succeed, expand, and hire more people. According to the Trump administration, they promised to eliminate two regulations for every new one, but actually wound up eliminating 8 old regulations for every 1 new regulation adopted.

Cutting taxes in an initiative that benefitted every tax bracket; providing the average American household an extra $3,100 every year.

A series of trade agreements and changes seen as beneficial to Americans, including replacing NAFTA with USMCA.

Finalized new trade agreement with South Korea.

Made a deal with the European Union to increase U.S. energy exports to Europe.

Secured $250 billion in new trade and investment deals in China and $12 billion in Vietnam.

Agreed to a new trade deal with Mexico & Canada that will increase jobs here and $$$ coming in.

Reached a breakthrough agreement with the E.U. to increase U.S. exports.

Imposed tariffs on China in response to China's forced technology transfer, intellectual property theft, and their chronically abusive trade practices, has agreed to a Part One trade deal with China.

Gave up to $12 billion in aid for farmers affected by unfair trade retaliation.

Instituted "Right to Try," allowing terminally ill patients to use potentially lifesaving, unproven treatments.

195

Prioritized and made permanent funding for historically black colleges.

Brokered peace deals or normalization agreements between Israel and five Muslim and Arab-Muslim countries.

Banned the teaching of "Critical Race Theory" in the federal government.

Withdrew from Iran nuclear deal.

Withdrew the United States from the job-killing Paris Climate Accord in 2017 and that same year the U.S. still led the world by having the largest reduction in Carbon emissions. Instituted a Buy American policy within federal agencies.

Achieved a $400 billion increase in contributions by NATO allies by 2024 with the number of members meeting their minimum obligations doubling.

Trump signed a bill making CBD and Hemp legal.

Trump's EPA gave $100 million to fix the water infrastructure problem in Flint, Michigan.

Trump signed a law ending the gag orders on pharmacists that prevented them from sharing money-saving information.

Trump signed the biggest wilderness protection & conservation bill in a decade and designated 375,000 acres as protected land.

Trump signed the Save our Seas Act which funds $10 million per year to clean tons of plastic & garbage from the ocean.

He signed a bill this year allowing some drug imports from Canada so that prescription prices would go down.

Trump signed an executive order this year that forces all healthcare providers to disclose the cost of their services so that Americans can comparison shop and know how much less providers charge insurance companies.

When signing that bill he said no American should be blindsided by bills for medical services they never agreed to in advance.

Hospitals will now be required to post their standard charges for services, which include the discounted price a hospital is willing to accept.

He created a White House VA Hotline to help veterans and principally staffed it with veterans and direct family members of veterans.

VA employees are being held accountable for poor performance, with more than 4,000 VA employees removed, demoted, and suspended so far.

Issued an executive order requiring the Secretaries of Defense, Homeland Security, and Veterans Affairs to submit a joint plan to provide veterans access to access to mental health treatment as they transition to civilian life.

Trump administration will provide HIV prevention drugs for free to 200,000 uninsured patients per year for 11 years.

Trump signed an order allowing small businesses to group together when buying insurance to get a better price.

In 2018, President Trump signed the groundbreaking First Step Act, a criminal justice bill which enacted reforms that make our justice system fairer and help former inmates successfully return to society. The First Step Act's reforms addressed inequities in sentencing laws that disproportionately harmed Black Americans and reformed mandatory minimums that created unfair outcomes.

Trump received the Bipartisan Justice Award at a historically black college for his criminal justice reform accomplishments.

The poverty rate fell to a 17-year low of 11.8% under the Trump administration as a result of a jobs-rich environment.

Poverty rates for African-Americans and Hispanic-Americans have reached their lowest levels since the U.S. began collecting such data.

President Trump signed a bill that creates five national monuments, expands several national parks, adds 1.3 million acres of wilderness, and permanently reauthorizes the Land and Water Conservation Fund.

Trump's USDA committed $124 Million to rebuild rural water infrastructure.

[Prior to the unexpected coronavirus pandemic] Consumer confidence & small business confidence is at an all time high.

[Prior to the unexpected coronavirus pandemic] More than 7 million jobs created since election.

[Prior to the unexpected coronavirus pandemic] More Americans were employed than ever recorded before in our history.

[Prior to the unexpected coronavirus pandemic] More than 400,000 manufacturing jobs created since his election.

Trump ordered Ric Grenell, his openly gay ambassador to Germany, to lead a global initiative to decriminalize homosexuality across the globe.

Through Trump's Anti-Trafficking Coordination Team (ACTeam) initiative, Federal law enforcement more than doubled convictions of human traffickers and increased the number of defendants charged by 75% in ACTeam districts.

President Trump has called on Congress to pass school choice legislation so that no child is trapped in a failing school because of his or her zip code.

The President signed funding legislation in September 2018 that increased funding for school choice by $42 million.

The tax cuts signed into law by President Trump promote school choice by allowing families to use 529 college savings plans for elementary and secondary education.

Signed the first Perkins CTE reauthorization since 2006, authorizing more than $1 billion for states each year to fund vocational and career education programs.

Executive order expanding apprenticeship opportunities for students and workers.

Trump issued an Executive Order prohibiting the U.S. government from discriminating against Christians or punishing expressions of faith.

Has had over a dozen US hostages freed, including those Obama could not get freed.

Trump signed the Music Modernization Act, the biggest change to copyright law in decades.

The Trump Administration is promoting second chance hiring to give former inmates the opportunity to live crime-free lives and find meaningful employment.

Trump's DOJ and the Board Of Prisons launched a new "Ready to Work Initiative" to help connect employers directly with former prisoners.

President Trump's historic tax cut legislation included new Opportunity Zone Incentives to promote investment in low-income communities across the country. 8,764 communities across the country have been designated as Opportunity Zones.

Trump directed the Education Secretary to end Common Core.

Trump signed the 9/11 Victims Compensation Fund into law.

Trump signed measure funding prevention programs for Veteran suicide.

Companies have brought back over a TRILLION dollars from overseas because of the TCJA bill that Trump signed.

[Prior to the coronavirus pandemic] manufacturing jobs were growing at the fastest rate in more than 30 years.

[Prior to the coronavirus pandemic] the stock market reached record highs.

[Prior to the coronavirus pandemic] Median household income hit highest level ever recorded.

[Prior to the coronavirus pandemic] African-American unemployment is at an all time low.

[Prior to the coronavirus pandemic] Hispanic-American unemployment is at an all time low.

[Prior to the coronavirus pandemic] Asian-American unemployment is at an all time low.

[Prior to the coronavirus pandemic] women's unemployment rate was at a 65-year low.

[Prior to the coronavirus pandemic] Youth unemployment is at a 50-year low.

[Prior to the coronavirus pandemic] He had the lowest unemployment rate ever recorded.

The Pledge to America's Workers has resulted in employers committing to train more than 4 million Americans.

Under Trump, the FDA approved more affordable generic drugs than ever before in history.

Reformed Medicare program to stop hospitals from overcharging low-income seniors on their drugs—saving seniors 100's of millions of $$$ this year alone.

Signed Right-To-Try legislation allowing terminally ill patients to try experimental treatment that wasn't allowed before.

Secured $6 billion in new funding to fight the opioid epidemic.

Signed VA Choice Act and VA Accountability Act, expanded VA telehealth services, walk-in-clinics, and same-day urgent primary and mental health care.

This is a partial list of accomplishments. Trump did all of this while fighting flagrant abuse and impeachment charges.

Historical Timeline of the United States of America

1000. Leif Ericson (Viking) discovers Vinland (New England).

1492. Columbus (Spain) discovers the New World.

1497. John Cabot (England) discovers the continent of North America.

1498. Columbus on third voyage discovers South America.

1506. Columbus dies at Valladolid, Spain.

1507. New World named after Amerigo Vespucci, Portuguese explorer.

1513. Balboa discovers the Pacific Ocean and Ponce de Leon discovers Florida.

1519-1521. Cortez conquers Mexico. Magellan sails round the world.

1524. Verrazano and Gomez explore New England coast.

1528. Cabeza do Vaca explores southern United States.

1533. Pizarro conquers Peru.

1534. Cartier (France) sails to the Gulf of St. Lawrence.

1541. Do Soto discovers the Mississippi River.

1565. Founding of St. Augustine, Florida.

1576. Frobisher discovers the northwest passage, Frobisher Strait.

1579. Drake (England) explores coast of California.

1584. Raleigh (England) sends first expedition to America.

1588. Defeat of the Spanish Armada. England replaced Spain as the dominant country in Europe and the New World.

1604. Acadia settled by the French.

1607. Founding of Jamestown, Virginia.

1608. Founding of Quebec by Champlain.

1609. Hudson discovers the Hudson River.

1619. First assembly meets at Jamestown, Slaves first sold in Virginia.

1620. Coming of the Pilgrims to Plymouth Rock in the Mayflower.

1623. Settlements at New Amsterdam, First settlements in New Hampshire.

1630. The great emigration to Massachusetts, The founding of Boston.

1634. Maryland first settled by Calvert.

1635. Connecticut settled by emigrants from Massachusetts.

1636. Founding of Providence by Roger Williams, Harvard College founded.

1637. War with Pequot Indians, First Black slaves in New England.

1638. Swedes first settle in Delaware.

1639. First constitution in America adopted by Connecticut.

1643. May 30. New England Confederation formed.

1649. Toleration Act in Maryland.

1655. Stuyvesant conquers the Swedes in Delaware.

1656. Quakers expelled from Massachusetts.

1662. Connecticut charter granted.

1663. Charter granted to Rhode Island, Charter for the Carolinas granted.

1664. The English conquer New Amsterdam, New Jersey given by King Charles II to his brother, the Duke of York.

1667. Fundamental Constitutions drawn up for the Carolinas.

1673. Marquette explores the Mississippi.

1676. Bacon's Rebellion in Virginia, King Philip's War in New England.

1681. Penn receives charter for Pennsylvania.

1682. Penn founds Philadelphia and makes treaty with the Indians, La Salle explores Louisiana and takes possession for France.

1686. Edmund Andros made governor of all New England.

1689. Rebellion against Andros; his fall and arrest.

1692. Salem witchcraft trials.

1700. Iberville plants colony in Louisiana.

1713. Treaty of Utrecht, ending Queen Anne's War, which began in 1702.

1733. Georgia settled by Oglethorpe.

1748. Treaty of Aix-la-Chapelle, ending King George's War, which began in 1744.

1754. Colonial Congress at Albany; Franklin's plan of union.

1755. Braddock's defeat.

1756. French and Indian War formally begun.

1759. Wolfe captures Quebec.

1763. Treaty of Paris; end of the war.

1765. Stamp Act, Colonial Congress in New York.

1770. "Boston Massacre."

1773. Destruction of tea in Boston Harbor.

1774. September 5. Continental Congress meets in Philadelphia, Boston Port Bill.

1775. April 19. Fight at Lexington and Concord, May 10, Capture of Ticonderoga, Meeting of Second Continental Congress at Philadelphia.

1775. June 17. Battle of Bunker Hill.

1776. July 4. Declaration of Independence, August 27. Battle of Long Island, December 26. Washington captures Hessians at Trenton.

1777. June 14. Flag of stars and stripes adopted by Congress, September 11. Battle of Brandywine, October 17. Surrender of Burgoyne, Washington encamps at Valley Forge and Howe occupies Philadelphia.

1778. French-American Alliance, June 28. Battle of Monmouth, December 29. British take Savannah.

1779. September 23. Naval victory of John Paul Jones.

1780. May 12. Charleston taken by British, August 16. Battle of Camden, October 7. Battle of King's Mountain.

1781. Adoption of the Articles of Confederation, October 19. Surrender of Cornwallis at Yorktown.

1782. November 30. Preliminary treaty of peace.

1783. September 3. Final treaty of peace signed, November 25. British army evacuates New York, December 4. Washington's farewell to his officers.

1786. Shays's rebellion in Massachusetts.

1787. Ordinance of 1787 adopted, May 14. Constitutional Convention meets at Philadelphia, Sept 17. Constitution finished and signed by the delegates.

1788. Rufus Putnam plants first settlement in Ohio, June 21. New Hampshire becomes the ninth state to ratify the Constitution, securing its adoption.

1789. March 4. New government goes into operation, April 30. Washington inaugurated first President.

1790. First census. Population 3,929,214.

1791. Vermont admitted to the Union. St. Clair defeated by the Indians

1792. Kentucky admitted to the Union.

1793. Thomas Jefferson founds Republican (Democratic) party.

1794. Wayne defeats the Indians in Battle of Fallen Timbers.

1795. Jay's treaty ratified.

1796. Tennessee admitted to the Union.

1797. John Adams inaugurated President.

1798. Alien and sedition laws enacted. Navy department established.

1798-1799. Kentucky and Virginia resolutions.

1798-1800. Serious trouble with France.

1799. December 14. Washington dies at Mt. Vernon.

1800. Overthrow of the Federal party, Capital removed to Washington, D.C.

1801. Jefferson becomes President.

1802. Ohio joins the Union.

1801-1805. War with the Barbary States, North Africa.

1803. Purchase of Louisiana.

1804. Burr kills Hamilton in a duel.

1805-1807. Lewis and Clarke expedition.

1806-1807. Burr's conspiracy, trial, and acquittal.

1807. Fulton succeeds with the steamboat, June 22. The Leopard fires on the Chesapeake, December. Jefferson's embargo enacted.

1808. Prohibition of the foreign slave trade.

1809. James Madison inaugurated President.

1811. November 7. Battle of Tippecanoe.

1812. June 18. War declared against England, August 16. Hull surrenders Detroit, August 19. The Constitution defeats the Guerriere, October 13. Battle of Queenstown Heights.

1813. September 10. Perry's victory on Lake Erie, October 5. Battle of the Thames, November 9. Battle of Talladega.

1814. July 25. Battle of Lundy's Lane, August 25. The British capture Washington, September 11. Battle at Plattsburg and defeat of the British on Lake Champlain, December. Hartford Convention, December 24. Treaty of Ghent.

1815. January 8. Battle of New Orleans, America secures indemnity and treaties from Algiers, Tunis, and Tripoli.

1816. Indiana admitted to the Union. Admission of Mississippi, 1817; of Illinois, 1818; of Alabama, 1819; of Maine, 1820; of Missouri, 1821.

1817. James Monroe becomes President.

1818. War with the Seminole Indians.

1819. Purchase of Florida from Spain, First steamship, the Savannah, crosses the Atlantic.

1820. The Missouri Compromise.

1823. December 2. Monroe Doctrine promulgated.

1825. Inauguration of John Quincy Adams. Opening of the Erie Canal, June 17. Lafayette lays corner stone of Bunker Hill Monument.

1826. July 4. Death of John Adams and Thomas Jefferson.

1828. Building of the first passenger railway begun at Baltimore.

1829. Andrew Jackson becomes President.

1830. Fifth census. Population 12,566,020.

1832. November 19. Nullification by South Carolina, Black Hawk War.

1833. Jackson removes bank deposits. Compromise tariff adopted.

1836. April 21. Battle of San Jacinto, Wilkes's Antarctic expedition, Admission of Arkansas.

1837. Inauguration of Van Buren, Patent of the telegraph by Morse, Admission of Michigan.

1841. March 4. William Henry Harrison inaugurated President; dies April 4, and John Tyler becomes President, Howe invents the sewing machine.

1844. First telegraph line in America, between Baltimore and Washington.

1845. James K. Polk becomes President. Florida and Texas admitted into the Union, Death of Andrew Jackson. 1846, Beginning of the Mexican War, Admission of Iowa, Walker tariff enacted, Wilmot Proviso introduced in Congress.

1847. February 23. Battle of Buena Vista, March 29. Capture of Vera Cruz by General Scott, September.Conquest of California.

1848. February. Treaty of Guadalupe Hidalgo, Discovery of gold in California, Wisconsin enters the Union.

1849. Zachary Taylor inaugurated President. 1850, Admission of California. Death of Calhoun July 9, Death of President Taylor. Millard Fillmore President, Clay Compromise enacted, Census shows population of 23,191,876.

1852. Death of Clay and Webster.

1853. Inauguration of Franklin Pierce.

1854. May. Kansas-Nebraska bill enacted.

1854. Commercial treaty with Japan.

1857. Inauguration of Buchanmi, March 6. Dred Scott decision.

1858. Admission of Minnesota, First Atlantic cable laid, Lincoln-Douglas debates, September 18. Mountain Meadow Massacre, Utah.

1859. Admission of Oregon, John Brown's raid on Harper's Ferry.

1860. Population 31,443,321.

1860. December 20. Secession of South Carolina.

1861. Secession of Mississippi on January 9; of Florida, January 10 Alabama, January 11; Georgia, January 19; Louisiana, January 26; Texas, February 1; Virginia, April 17; Arkansas, May 6; North Carolina, May 20; Tennessee, June 8, February 4. Confederate government organized, March 4. Lincoln inaugurated President of the United States, April 14. Fall of Fort Sumter, July 21. Battle of Bull Run, November 8. Capture of Mason and Slidell, Admission of Kansas.

1862. February 16. Surrender of Fort Donelson, March 9. Duel between the Monitor and the Merrimac, April 6-7. Battle of Shiloh, April 16. Slavery abolished in District of Columbia, April 25. Farragut captures New Orleans, July 1. Battle of Malvern Hill; last of the seven days' battle before Richmond, August 30. Second Battle of Bull Run, September 17. Battle of Antietam, December 13. Battle of Fredericksburg.

1863. January 1. Lincoln issues Emancipation Proclamation, January 2. Battle of Murfreesboro, Admission of West Virginia, May 2. Battle of Chancellorsville, July 14. Battle of Gettysburg, July 4. Surrender of Vicksburg, September 19-20. Battle of Chickamauga, November 19. Lincoln's address at Gettysburg, November 24-25. Battle of Chattanooga.

1864. May 6. Battle of the Wilderness, May 11. Battle of Spottsylvania, June 19. The Kearsarge sinks the Alabama, August 5. Battle of Mobile Bay, September 2. Sherman captures Atlanta, October 19. Battle of Cedar Creek, November 15. Sherman begins his march to the sea, December 15-16. Battle of Nashville, Admission of Nevada.

1865. April 1. Battle of Five Forks, April 3. Evacuation of Richmond, April 9. Surrender of Lee at Appomattox, April 14. Assassination of Lincoln; Andrew Johnson President, April 26. Surrender of Johnston's army, December 18. Thirteenth Amendment ratified.

1866. July 27. Second Atlantic cable completed.

1867. May 2. Reconstruction bill passed over veto, Purchase of Alaska, Admission of Nebraska

1868. February 24. President Johnson impeached by the House, Trial in the Senate fails, July 21. Fourteenth Amendment adopted.

1869. Inauguration of U. S. Grant, May 10. Pacific Railroad completed.

211

1870. Population 38,558,371, March 30. Fifteenth Amendment ratified.

1871. November. Great fire in Chicago.

1873. February. Congress demonetizes silver.

1876. Centennial Exposition at Philadeiphia, Admission of Colorado, Invention of the telephone, Custer's army destroyed by the Indians.

1877. Inauguration of R. B. Hayes, Great railroad strike.

1878. Electric light perfected, Bland-Allison silver bill passed.

1879. January 1. Resumption of specie payments

1880. Population 50,155,783.

1881. James A. Garfield inaugurated President, July 2. Assassination of Garfield. Dies September 19, Chester A. Arthur becomes President.

1883. Letter postage reduced to two cents.

1885. Grover Cleveland becomes President.

1886. October 6. Statue of Liberty unveiled, New York.

1886. Presidential Succession Law enacted.

1889. Benjamin Harrison becomes President, Oklahoma opened to settlers, North Dakota, South Dakota, Montana, and Washington admitted into the Union.

1890. Population 62,622,250, Idaho and Wyoming admitted, McKinley tariff enacted, Sherman silver law passed.

1891. Chilians assault American sailors at Valparsiso.

1893. World's Columbian Exposition at Chicago.

1894. Wilson tariff law enacted.

1895. December 17. Cleveland issues his Venezuelan message.

1897. William McKinley becomes President, July 24. Dingley tariff becomes law.

1898. February 15. Destruction of the Maine at Havana, Congress declares war against Spain (existing from April 21), May 1. Battle of Manila, July 1-3. Battle of San Juan, Battle of Santiago, Annexation of Hawaii, August 12. Peace protocol signed, December 10. Treaty with Spain signed at Paris.

1899. May 18. Peace Conference meets at The Hague, Samoan treaty made by the United States, Great Britain, and Germany.

1900 Galveston hurricane leaves an estimated 6,000 to 8,000 dead (Sept. 8). According to the census, the nation's population numbers nearly 76 million.

1901 McKinley's second inauguration (March 4). He is shot (Sept. 6) by anarchist Leon Czolgosz in Buffalo, N.Y., and later dies from his wounds (Sept. 14). He is succeeded by his vice president, Theodore Roosevelt.

1903 U.S. acquires Panama Canal Zone (treaty signed Nov. 17). Wright brothers make the first controlled, sustained flight in heavier-than-air aircraft at Kitty Hawk, N.C. (Dec. 17).

1905 Theodore Roosevelt's second inauguration (March 4).

1906 San Francisco earthquake leaves 500 dead or missing and destroys about 4 sq mi of the city (April 18).

1908 Bureau of Investigation, forerunner of the FBI, is established (July 26).

1909 William Howard Taft is inaugurated as the 27th president (March 4). Mrs. Taft has 80 Japanese cherry trees planted along the banks of the Potomac River.

1913 Woodrow Wilson is inaugurated as the 28th president (March 4). Seventeenth Amendment to the Constitution is ratified, providing for the direct election of U.S. senators by popular vote rather than by the state legislatures (April 8). The Federal Reserve formed (Dec 10).

1914–1918 World War I: U.S. enters World War I, declaring war on Germany (April 6, 1917) and Austria-Hungary (Dec. 7, 1917) three years after conflict began in 1914. Armistice ending World War I is signed (Nov. 11, 1918).

1914 Panama Canal opens to traffic (Aug. 15).

1915 First long distance telephone service, between New York and San Francisco, is demonstrated (Jan. 25).

1916 U.S. agrees to purchase Danish West Indies (Virgin Islands) for $25 million (treaty signed Aug. 14). Jeannette Rankin of Montana is the first woman elected to the U.S. House of Representatives (Nov. 7).

1917 Wilson's second inauguration (March 5). First regular airmail service begins, with one round trip a day between Washington, DC, and New York (May 15).

1918 Worldwide influenza epidemic strikes; by 1920, nearly 20 million are dead. In U.S., 500,000 perish.

1919 League of Nations meets for the first time; U.S. is not represented (Jan. 13). Eighteenth Amendment to the Constitution is ratified, prohibiting the manufacture, sale, and transportation of liquor (Jan. 16). It is later repealed by the Twenty-First Amendment in 1933. Nineteenth Amendment to the Constitution is ratified, granting women the right to vote (Aug. 18). President Wilson suffers a stroke (Sept. 26). Treaty of Versailles, outlining terms for peace at the end of World War I, is rejected by the Senate (Nov. 19).

1921 Warren G. Harding is inaugurated as the 29th president (March 4). He signs resolution declaring peace with Austria and Germany (July 2).

1923 President Harding dies suddenly (Aug. 2). He is succeeded by his vice president, Calvin Coolidge. Teapot Dome scandal breaks, as Senate launches an investigation into improper leasing of naval oil reserves during Harding administration (Oct.)

1925 Coolidge's second inauguration (March 4). Tennessee passes a law against the teaching of evolution in public schools (March 23), setting the stage for the Scopes Monkey Trial (July 10–25).

1927 Charles Lindbergh makes the first solo nonstop transatlantic flight in his plane The Spirit of St. Louis (May 20–21).

1929 Herbert Hoover is inaugurated as the 31st president (March 4). Stock market crash precipitates the Great Depression (Oct. 29).

1931 The Star-Spangled Banner is adopted as the national anthem (March 3).

1932 Hattie Wyatt Caraway of Arkansas is the first woman elected to the U.S. Senate, to fill a vacancy caused by the death of her husband (Jan. 12). She is

215

reelected in 1932 and 1938. Amelia Earhart completes first solo nonstop transatlantic flight by a woman (May 21).

1933 Twentieth Amendment to the Constitution, sometimes called the "Lame Duck Amendment," is ratified, moving the president's inauguration date from March 4 to Jan. 20 (Jan. 23). Franklin Roosevelt is inaugurated as the 32nd president (March 4). New Deal recovery measures are enacted by Congress (March 9–June 16). Twenty-First Amendment to the Constitution is ratified, repealing Prohibition (Dec. 5).

1935 Works Progress Administration is established (April 8). Social Security Act is passed (Aug. 14). Bureau of Investigation (established 1908) becomes the Federal Bureau of Investigation under J. Edgar Hoover

1937 F. Roosevelt's second inauguration (Jan. 20).

1938 Fair Labor Standards Act is passed, setting the first minimum wage in the U.S. at 25 cents per hour (June 25).

1939–1945 World War II: U.S. declares its neutrality in European conflict (Sept. 5, 1939). F. Roosevelt's third inauguration (Jan. 20, 1941). He is the first and only president elected to a third term. Japan attacks Hawaii, Guam, and the Philippines (Dec. 7, 1941). U.S. declares war on Japan (Dec. 8). Germany and Italy declare war on the United States; U.S. reciprocates by declaring war on both countries (Dec. 11). Allies invade North Africa (Oct.–Dec. 1942) and Italy (Sept.–Dec. 1943). Allies invade France on D-Day (June 6, 1944). F. Roosevelt's fourth inauguration (Jan. 20, 1945). President Roosevelt, Churchill, and Stalin meet at Yalta in the USSR to discuss postwar occupation of Germany (Feb. 4–11). President Roosevelt dies of a stroke (April 12) and is succeeded by his vice president, Harry Truman. Germany surrenders unconditionally (May 7). Bretton

Woods Conference, IMF and the World Bank are formed July 1-22). First atomic bomb is detonated at Alamogordo, N.M. (July 16). President Truman, Churchill, and Stalin meet at Potsdam, near Berlin, Germany, to demand Japan's unconditional surrender and to discuss plans for postwar Europe (July 17–Aug. 2). U.S. drops atomic bomb on Hiroshima, Japan (Aug. 6). U.S. drops atomic bomb on Nagasaki, Japan (Aug. 9). Japan agrees to unconditional surrender (Aug. 14). Japanese envoys sign surrender terms aboard the USS Missouri in Tokyo harbor (Sept. 2).

1945 United Nations is established (Oct. 24).

1946 The Philippines, which had been ceded to the U.S. by Spain at the end of the Spanish-American War, becomes an independent republic (July 4).

1947 Presidential Succession Act is signed into law by President Truman (July 18). Central Intelligence Agency is established.

1948 Congress passes foreign aid bill including the Marshall Plan, which provides for European postwar recovery (April 2). Soviets begin blockade of Berlin in the first major crisis of the cold war (June 24). In response, U.S. and Great Britain begin airlift of food and fuel to West Berlin (June 26).

1949 Truman's second inauguration (Jan. 20). North Atlantic Treaty Organization (NATO) is established (April 4). Soviets end blockade of Berlin (May 12), but airlift continues until Sept. 30.

1950–1953 Korean War: Cold war conflict between Communist and non-Communist forces on Korean Peninsula. North Korean communists invade South Korea (June 25, 1950). President Truman, without the approval of Congress, commits American troops to battle (June 27). President Truman removes Gen.

Douglas MacArthur as head of U.S. Far East Command (April 11, 1951). Armistice agreement is signed (July 27, 1953).

1955–1975 Vietnam War: Prolonged conflict between Communist forces of North Vietnam, backed by China and the USSR, and non-Communist forces of South Vietnam, backed by the United States. President Truman authorizes $15 million in economic and military aid to the French, who are fighting to retain control of French Indochina, including Vietnam. As part of the aid package, Truman also sends 35 military advisers (May 1955). North Vietnamese torpedo boats allegedly attack U.S. destroyer in Gulf of Tonkin off the coast of North Vietnam (Aug. 2, 1964). Congress approves Gulf of Tonkin resolution, authorizing President Johnson to take any measures necessary to defend U.S. forces and prevent further aggression (Aug. 7). U.S. planes begin bombing raids of North Vietnam (Feb. 1965). First U.S. combat troops arrive in South Vietnam (March 8–9). North Vietnamese army and Viet Cong launch Tet Offensive, attacking Saigon and other key cities in South Vietnam (Jan.–Feb. 1968). American soldiers kill 300 Vietnamese villagers in My Lai massacre (March 16). U.S. troops invade Cambodia (May 1, 1970). Representatives of North and South Vietnam, the Viet Cong, and the U.S. sign a cease-fire agreement in Paris (Jan. 27, 1973). Last U.S. troops leave Vietnam (March 29). South Vietnamese government surrenders to North Vietnam; U.S. embassy Marine guards and last U.S. civilians are evacuated (April 30, 1975).

1951 Twenty-Second Amendment to the Constitution is ratified, limiting the president to two terms (Feb. 27). President Truman speaks in first coast-to-coast live television broadcast (Sept. 4).

1952 Puerto Rico becomes a U.S. commonwealth (July 25). First hydrogen bomb is detonated by the U.S. on Eniwetok, an atoll in the Marshall Islands (Nov. 1).

1953 Dwight Eisenhower is inaugurated as the 34th president (Jan. 20). Julius and Ethel Rosenberg are executed for passing secret information about U.S. atomic weaponry to the Soviets (June 19).

1954 Sen. Joseph R. McCarthy accuses army officials, members of the media, and other public figures of being Communists during highly publicized hearings (April 22–June 17). Brown v. Board of Education of Topeka, Kans.: Landmark Supreme Court decision declares that racial segregation in schools is unconstitutional (May 17).

1957 Eisenhower's second inauguration (Jan. 21). President sends federal troops to Central High School in Little Rock, Ark., to enforce integration of black students (Sept. 24).

1958 Explorer I, first American satellite, is launched (Jan. 31).

1959 Alaska becomes the 49th state (Jan. 3) and Hawaii becomes the 50th (Aug. 21).

1961 U.S. severs diplomatic relations with Cuba (Jan. 3). John F. Kennedy is inaugurated as the 35th president (Jan. 20). Bay of Pigs invasion of Cuba fails (April 17–20). A mixed-race group of volunteers sponsored by the Committee on Racial Equality—the so-called Freedom Riders—travel on buses through the South in order to protest racially segregated interstate bus facilities (May).

1962 Lt. Col. John Glenn becomes first U.S. astronaut to orbit Earth (Feb. 20). Cuban Missile Crisis: President Kennedy denounces Soviet Union for secretly installing missile bases on Cuba and initiates a naval blockade of the island (Oct. 22–Nov. 20).

1963 Rev. Martin Luther King, Jr., delivers his "I Have a Dream" speech before a crowd of 200,000 during the civil rights march on Washington, DC (Aug. 28). President Kennedy is assassinated in Dallas, Tex. (Nov. 22). He is succeeded in office by his vice president, Lyndon B. Johnson.

1964 President Johnson signs the Civil Rights Act (July 2).

1965 In his annual state of the Union address, President Johnson proposes his "Great Society" program (Jan. 4). L. Johnson's second inauguration (Jan. 20). State troopers attack peaceful demonstrators led by Rev. Martin Luther King, Jr., as they try to cross bridge in Selma, Ala. (March 7). President Johnson signs the Voting Rights Act, which prohibits discriminatory voting practices (Aug. 6). In six days of rioting in Watts, a black section of Los Angeles, 35 people are killed and 883 injured (Aug. 11–16).

1966 Miranda v. Arizona: Landmark Supreme Court decision further defines due process clause of Fourteenth Amendment and establishes Miranda rights (June 13).

1967 Twenty-Fifth Amendment to the Constitution is ratified, outlining the procedures for filling vacancies in the presidency and vice presidency (Feb. 10).

1968 Rev. Martin Luther King, Jr., is assassinated in Memphis, Tenn. (April 4). Sen. Robert F. Kennedy is assassinated in Los Angeles, Calif. (June 5–6).

1969 Richard Nixon is inaugurated as the 37th president (Jan. 20). Astronauts Neil Armstrong and Edwin Aldrin, Jr., become the first men to land on the Moon (July 20).

1970 Four students are shot to death by National Guardsmen during an antiwar protest at Kent State University (May 1).

1971 The Twenty-Sixth Amendment to the Constitution is ratified, lowering the voting age from 21 to 18 (July 1).

1972 Nixon makes historic visit to Communist China (Feb. 21–27). U.S. and Soviet Union sign strategic arms control agreement known as SALT I (May 26). Five men, all employees of Nixon's reelection campaign, are caught breaking into rival Democratic headquarters at the Watergate complex in Washington, DC (June 17).

1973 Nixon's second inauguration (Jan. 20). Roe v. Wade: Landmark Supreme Court decision legalizes abortion in first trimester of pregnancy (Jan. 22). Senate Select Committee begins televised hearings to investigate Watergate cover-up (May 17–Aug. 7). Vice President Spiro T. Agnew resigns over charges of corruption and income tax evasion (Oct. 10). President Nixon nominates Gerald R. Ford as vice president (Oct. 12). Ford is confirmed by Congress and sworn in (Dec. 6). He is the first vice president to succeed to the office under the terms laid out by the Twenty-Fifth Amendment.

1974 House Judiciary Committee recommends to full House that Nixon be impeached on grounds of obstruction of justice, abuse of power, and contempt of Congress (July 27–30). Nixon resigns; he is succeeded in office by his vice president, Gerald Ford (Aug. 9). Nixon is granted an unconditional pardon by President Ford (Sept. 8). Five former Nixon aides go on trial for their involvement in the Watergate cover-up (Oct. 15); H. R. Haldeman, John D. Ehrlichman, and John Mitchell eventually serve time in prison. Nelson Rockefeller is confirmed and sworn in as vice president (Dec. 19).

1977 Jimmy Carter is inaugurated as the 39th president (Jan. 20). President Carter signs treaty (Sept. 7) agreeing to turn control of Panama Canal over to Panama on Dec. 31, 1999.

1978 President Carter meets with Egyptian president Anwar Sadat and Israeli prime minister Menachem Begin at Camp David (Sept. 6); Sadat and Begin sign Camp David Accord, ending 30-year conflict between Egypt and Israel (Sept. 17).

1979 U.S. establishes diplomatic ties with mainland China for the first time since Communist takeover in 1949 (Jan. 1). Malfunction at Three Mile Island nuclear reactor in Pennsylvania causes near meltdown (March 28). Panama takes control of the Canal Zone, formerly administered by U.S. (Oct. 1). Iranian students storm U.S. embassy in Teheran and hold 66 people hostage (Nov. 4); 13 of the hostages are released (Nov. 19–20).

1980 President Carter announces that U.S. athletes will not attend Summer Olympics in Moscow unless Soviet Union withdraws from Afghanistan (Jan. 20). FBI's undercover bribery investigation, code named Abscam, implicates a U.S. senator, seven members of the House, and 31 other public officials (Feb. 2). U.S. mission to rescue hostages in Iran is aborted after a helicopter and cargo plane collide at the staging site in a remote part of Iran and 8 servicemen are killed (April 25).

1981 Ronald Reagan is inaugurated as the 40th president (Jan. 20). U.S. hostages held in Iran are released after 444 days in captivity (Jan. 20). President Reagan is shot in the chest by John Hinckley, Jr. (March 30). Sandra Day O'Connor is sworn in as the first woman Supreme Court justice (Sept. 25).

1982 Deadline for ratification of the Equal Rights Amendment to the Constitution passes without the necessary votes (June 30).

1983 U.S. invades Caribbean island of Grenada after a coup by Marxist faction in the government (Oct. 25).

1985 Reagan's second inauguration (Jan. 21).

1986 Space shuttle Challenger explodes 73 seconds after liftoff, killing all seven crew members (Jan. 28). It is the worst accident in the history of the U.S. space program. U.S. bombs military bases in Libya in effort to deter terrorist strikes on American targets (April 14). Iran-Contra scandal breaks when White House is forced to reveal secret arms-for-hostages deals (Nov.).

1987 Congress holds public hearings in Iran-Contra investigation (May 5–Aug. 3). In a speech in Berlin, President Reagan challenges Soviet leader Mikhail Gorbachev to "tear down this wall" and open Eastern Europe to political and economic reform (June 12). Reagan and Gorbachev sign INF treaty, the first arms-control agreement to reduce the superpowers' nuclear weapons (Dec. 8).

1989 George H. W. Bush is inaugurated as the 41st president (Jan. 20). Oil tanker Exxon Valdez runs aground in Prince William Sound, spilling more than 10 million gallons of oil (March 24). It is the largest oil spill in U.S. history. President Bush signs legislation to provide for federal bailout of nearly 800 insolvent savings and loan institutions (Aug. 9). U.S. forces invade Panama in an attempt to capture Gen. Manuel Noriega, who previously had been indicted in the U.S. on drug trafficking charges (Dec. 20).

1990 Iraqi troops invade Kuwait, leading to the Persian Gulf War (Aug. 2).

1991 Persian Gulf War: U.S. leads international coalition in military operation (code named "Desert Storm") to drive Iraqis out of Kuwait (Jan. 16–Feb. 28). Iraq accepts terms of UN ceasefire, marking an end of the war (April 6).

1991 U.S. and Soviet Union sign START I treaty, agreeing to further reduce strategic nuclear arms (July 31). Senate Judiciary Committee conducts televised hearings to investigate allegations of past sexual harassment brought against Supreme Court nominee Clarence Thomas by Anita Hill, a law professor at the University of Oklahoma (Oct. 11–13).

1992 Following the breakup of the Soviet Union in Dec. 1991, President Bush and Russian president Boris Yeltsin meet at Camp David and formally declare an end to the cold war (Feb. 1). The acquittal of four white police officers charged in the 1991 beating of black motorist Rodney King in Los Angeles sets off several days of rioting, leading to more than 50 deaths, thousands of injuries and arrests, and $1 billion in property damage (April 29). President Bush authorizes sending U.S. troops to Somalia as part of UN relief effort (Dec. 4). President Bush grants pardons to six officials convicted or indicted in the Iran-Contra scandal, leading some to suspect a cover-up (Dec. 24).

1993 Bill Clinton is inaugurated as the 42nd president (Jan. 20). Bomb explodes in basement garage of World Trade Center, killing 6, injuring 1,000, and causing more than $500 million in damage (Feb. 26). After 51-day standoff with federal agents, Branch Davidian compound in Waco, Tex., burns to the ground, killing 80 cult members (April 19). President Clinton orders missile attack against Iraq in retaliation for alleged plot to assassinate former President Bush (June 26). Eighteen U.S. soldiers are killed in ambush by Somali militiamen in Mogadishu

(Oct. 3–4). President Clinton signs North American Free Trade Agreement into law (Dec. 8).

1994 Paula Jones, a former Arkansas state employee, files a federal lawsuit against President Clinton for sexual harassment (May 6).

1995 Bombing of federal office building in Oklahoma City kills 168 people (April 19). U.S. establishes full diplomatic relations with Vietnam (July 11). President Clinton sends first 8,000 of 20,000 U.S. troops to Bosnia for 12-month peacekeeping mission (Dec.). Budget standoff between President Clinton and Congress results in partial shutdown of U.S. government (Dec. 16–Jan. 6).

1997 Clinton's second inauguration (Jan. 20).

1998 President Clinton denies having had a sexual relationship with a White House intern named Monica Lewinsky (Jan. 17). President Clinton releases 1999 federal budget plan; it is the first balanced budget since 1969 (Feb. 2). In televised address, President Clinton admits having had a sexual relationship with Monica Lewinsky (Aug. 17). U.S. launches missile attacks on targets in Sudan and Afghanistan following terrorist attacks on U.S. embassies in Kenya and Tanzania (Aug. 20). U.S. and Britain launch air strikes against weapons sites in Iraq (Dec. 16). House of Representatives votes to impeach President Clinton on charges of perjury and obstruction of justice (Dec. 19).

1999 Senate acquits Clinton of impeachment charges (Feb. 12). NATO wages air campaign against Yugoslavia over killing and deportation of ethnic Albanians in Kosovo (March 24–June 10). School shooting at Columbine High School in Littleton, Colo., leaves 14 students (including the 2 shooters) and 1 teacher dead and 23 others wounded (April 20). U.S. and China sign historic trade agreement (Nov. 15).

225

2000 - According to the census, the nation's population numbers more than 280 million (April 1). No clear winner is declared in the close presidential election contest between Vice President Al Gore and Texas governor George W. Bush (Nov. 7). More than a month after the presidential election, the U.S. Supreme Court rules against a manual recount of ballots in certain Florida counties, which it contends would violate the Constitution's equal protection and due process guarantees. The decision provokes enormous controversy, with critics maintaining that the court has in effect determined the outcome of the election (Dec. 12). Bush formally accepts the presidency, having won a slim majority in the electoral college but not a majority of the popular vote (Dec. 13).

2001- George W. Bush is inaugurated as the 43rd president (Jan. 20). Two hijacked jetliners ram twin towers of World Trade Center in worst terrorist attack against U.S.; a third hijacked plane flies into the Pentagon, and a fourth crashes in rural Pennsylvania. More than 3,000 people die in the attacks (Sept. 11). U.S. and Britain launch air attacks against targets in Afghanistan after Taliban government fails to hand over Saudi terrorist Osama bin Laden, the suspected mastermind behind the Sept. 11 attacks (Oct. 7). Following air campaign and ground assault by Afghani opposition troops, the Taliban regime topples (Dec. 9); however, the hunt for Bin Laden and other members of al-Qaeda terrorist organization continues.

2002 - In his first State of the Union address, President Bush labels Iran, Iraq, and North Korea an "axis of evil" and declares that U.S. will wage war against states that develop weapons of mass destruction (Jan. 29). President Bush signs legislation creating a new cabinet department of Homeland Security. (Nov. 25).

2003 - Space shuttle Columbia explodes upon reentry into Earth's atmosphere, killing all seven astronauts on board (Feb. 1). War waged by the U.S. and Britain against Iraq begins (March 19). President Bush signs $350 billion tax-cut bill (May 28).

2004 - The U.S. returns sovereignty to an interim government in Iraq, but maintains roughly 135,000 troops in the country to fight a growing insurgency (June 28). Four hurricanes devastate Florida and other parts of the southern United States (Aug. and Sept.).

2005 - The U.S. engagement in Iraq continues amid that country's escalating violence and fragile political stability. Hurricane Katrina wreaks catastrophic damage on Mississippi and Louisiana; 80% of New Orleans is flooded (Aug. 29–30). All levels of government are criticized for the delayed and inadequate response to the disaster. Sandra Day O'Connor announces her retirement as a Supreme Court Justice (July 1). Chief Justice William H Rehnquist passes away after battling thyroid cancer (Sept. 3). John G. Roberts assumes the role of chief justice (Sept. 29). Stryker Brigade Combat Team Soldiers from Company A, 1st Battalion, 24th Infantry Regiment, 1st Brigade, 25th Infantry Division, search for insurgents during Operation Indy in Mosul, Iraq.

2006 - The U.S. Census Bureau estimates that the population of the United States has reached 300 million (Oct. 17).

2007 - California Democrat Nancy Pelosi becomes the first woman Speaker of the House of Representatives (Jan. 4). Attorney General Alberto Gonzales admits that the Justice Department made mistakes and exercised poor judgment in firing nine federal prosecutors in late 2006 (March 13). Male student kills two in a Virginia Tech dorm. Two hours later, he kills 30 more in a classroom building before committing suicide. The shooting rampage is the most deadly in U.S. history. Fifteen others are wounded (April 16). The minimum wage in the U.S. increases to $5.85, up from $5.15. It's the first increase in 10 years. The wage will increase 70 cents each year through 2009, when it reaches $7.25 an hour (July 24). An eight-lane interstate bridge in Minneapolis, Minnesota, that is packed with cars breaks into sections and falls into the river, killing 13 people (Aug. 1). The White House announces that Alberto Gonzales, the beleaguered attorney general, has submitted his resignation to President Bush (Aug. 27). In highly anticipated testimony, Gen. David Petraeus tells members of the House Foreign Affairs and Armed Services committees that the U.S. military needs more time to meet its goals in Iraq. Petraeus rejects suggestions that the U.S. shift from a counterinsurgency operation to training Iraqi forces and fighting terrorists. Instead, he says the U.S. must continue all three missions (Sep 10).

2008 - After months of campaigning and primary races, Barack Obama and John McCain are finally chosen as the presidential nominees for the Democratic and Republican parties, respectively (June 3). After months of unraveling, the economy finally comes crashing down in 2008, with the Dow Jones Industrial Average tumbling 4.4% in one day, Lehman Brothers filing for bankruptcy, and Bush putting mortgage giants Fannie Mae and Freddie Mac under government conservatorship (Sept.). Democrats perform well across the board in the November elections. Barack Obama becomes the first African-American to be elected President, with 52.8% of the vote. In Congress, Democrats retain majorities in both the House and the Senate, with 57 Senators and 178 Representatives (Nov. 4).

2009 - President Obama signs executive orders closing all secret prisons and detention camps run by the CIA, including the infamous Guantanamo Bay prison in Cuba, and banning coercive interrogation methods (Jan. 22). The Senate votes in

228

favor of a $168 billion package that gives rebates of $300-$600 for individuals earning up to $75,000 and to couples with incomes up to $150,000. Families will be eligible for up to $300 in rebates for each child (Feb. 7). President Obama signs the $787 billion stimulus package into law. The president's hope is that the package will create 3.5 million jobs for Americans in the next two years (Feb. 17). Insurance giant American International Group reports a $61.7 billion loss for the fourth quarter of 2008. A.I.G. lost $99.3 billion in 2008. The federal government, which has already provided the company with a $60 billion loan, will be giving A.I.G. an additional $30 billion. Nearly 80% of A.I.G. is now owned by the federal government (March 2). After confirming 20 cases of swine flu in the United States, including eight in New York City, the U.S. declares the outbreak a public health emergency (April 26). Michael Jackson, lifelong musician, pop singer, and superstar, dies at age 50 (June 25). The Senate approves, 68 to 31, the nomination of Sonia Sotomayor to the U.S. Supreme Court. She's the first Hispanic Supreme Court justice and the third woman to serve on the Court. (Aug. 25) Senator Edward "Ted" Kennedy, a fixture in the Senate for 46 years, dies of brain cancer at the age of 77 (Aug. 6). Oscar Grant race riots take place in Oakland, California. A shooting at the Fort Hood army post in Texas kills 13 and injures 29. Ten of those killed are military personnel. Maj. Nidal Malik Hasan, an army psychiatrist, is charged with 13 counts of premeditated murder (Nov. 5). A Nigerian man on a flight from Amsterdam to Detroit allegedly attempted to ignite an explosive device hidden in his underwear. The alleged bomber, Umar Farouk Abdulmutallab, told officials later that he was directed by the terrorist group Al Qaeda (Dec. 25).

2010 - An explosion and fire on the Deepwater Horizon oil rig in the Gulf of Mexico sends millions of gallons of oil into the sea. The spill kills 11 and is the largest off-shore spill in U.S. history as well as one of the largest spills in world history (Jan. 22). The United States Senate votes 63 to 37 to confirm President Obama's most recent nominee to the U.S. Supreme Court, Elena Kagan, as the newest Justice. Kagan is only the fourth woman to ever hold this position, and she'll be the third female member of the current bench, joining Ruth Bader Ginsburg and Sonia Sotomayor. Kagan is the former dean of Harvard Law School; she'll be the only member of the current Supreme Court to have no previous experience as a judge (Aug. 5). The Senate votes 65 to 31 in favor of repealing Don't Ask, Don't Tell, the Clinton-era military policy that forbids openly gay men and women from serving in the military. Eight Republicans side with the Democrats to strike down the ban. The repeal is sent to President Obama for his final signature. The ban will not be lifted officially until Obama, Defense Secretary Robert Gates, and Admiral Mike Mullen, the chairman of the Joint Chiefs of Staff, agree that the military is ready to enact the change and that it won't affect military readiness (Dec. 18).

2011 - Arizona Representative Gabrielle Giffords is among 17 shot by a gunman who opened fire on the congresswoman's constituent meeting outside a local grocery store. The gunman, who police identify as Jared Lee Loughner, is apprehended (Jan. 8). President Obama announces his intention to reduce the federal deficit by $400 billion over 10 years. His plan for enacting this dramatic reduction includes budget cuts and freezes, including a spending freeze on many domestic programs (Jan. 24). The Obama Administration determines that the Defense of Marriage Act is unconstitutional. The Justice Department will stop defending the law in court (Feb. 23). With less than two hours to spare, an agreement on the federal budget is made, avoiding a government shutdown. Republicans demand a provision to restrict financing to Planned Parenthood and other groups that provide abortions. Obama and the Democrats refuse to budge on the abortion provision, but they do agree to tens of billions in spending cuts (April 1). Legendary Boston crime boss, James "Whitey" Bulger is found and arrested by federal authorities in Santa Monica, Calif. Bulger is on the FBI's 10 Most Wanted list and has been indicted in 19 murders (June 22). Congress makes an 11th-hour deal to prevent a national default. The deal raises the debt ceiling in two steps to $2.4 trillion and cuts an initial $1 trillion in spending over ten years (Aug. 1). For the first time in history, the U.S. has its credit rating lowered. Credit agency Standard & Poor's lowered the nation's credit rating from the top grade of AAA to AA+, removing the U.S. from its list of risk-free borrowers (Aug. 5). The Congressional Supercommittee in charge of finding $1.2 trillion in deficit reductions fails to agree on what programs to cut. Therefore, automatic cuts to military and domestic programs will go into effect in 2013 (Nov. 21).

2012 - The Pentagon announces that women will now be permanently assigned to battalions. Many women already serve in those battalions due to demand in Iraq and Afghanistan. The new ruling only makes these job assignments official and upholds the ban on women serving in combat (Feb. 9). Hurricane Sandy causes at least 132 deaths and an estimated 82 billion in damages, making it the second costliest hurricane in the U.S., behind Katrina. New Jersey, New York, and Connecticut are hardest hit (Oct. 29). President Obama is re-elected, narrowly defeating Republican nominee Mitt Romney. Democrats keep their majority in the Senate. Key victories for the Democrats include a win for Tammy Baldwin in Wisconsin. Her victory makes her the first openly gay candidate to capture a seat in the Senate. The Republicans keep the majority in the House of Representatives with 232 seats to 191 for the Democrats (Nov. 6). Manual Diaz race riots take place in Los Angeles, California. Adam Lanza, age 20, forces his way into Sandy Hook Elementary School, in Newtown, Connecticut, and kills 26 people, including

20 children between the ages of six and seven. Then Lanza takes his own life while still inside the school (Dec. 14).

2013 - Multiple bombs explode near the finish line of the Boston Marathon. Three people are killed and more than 170 people are injured. Kimini Gray race riots break out in Brooklyn, New York. (April 15). The Guardian receives information that reveals that the National Security Agency (NSA) is using PRISM to spy on the web activities, including email, of U.S. citizens. Through PRISM, a clandestine national security surveillance program, the NSA has direct access to Facebook, YouTube, Skype, Google, Apple, Yahoo and other websites (June 6). The Guardian publishes a report on another NSA tool called Boundless Informant, used by the U.S. government to watch activity in every country in the world. President Obama confirms the existence of PRISM and its use to spy on the online activity of U.S. citizens (June 8). Edward Snowden, a former CIA employee, comes forward and admits that he is the source of the recent NSA leaks (June 9). Congress fails to agree on a budget and pass a spending bill, causing the government to shut down. The government shutdown forces about 800,000 federal workers off the job (Oct. 1). The night before the debt ceiling deadline, both the House and Senate approve a bill to fund the government until January 15, 2014, and raise the debt limit through February 7, 2014. The bill ends the 16-day government shutdown. It also ends the Republican standoff with President Obama over the Affordable Care Act (Oct. 16). The Senate deploys the "nuclear option," voting 52-48 to end the right of the minority to filibuster executive and judicial branch nominees. The vote is called a monumental, once in a generation change to Senate procedure (Nov. 21). The first ruling against the NSA surveillance program is handed down by Judge Richard Leon of Federal District Court for the District of Columbia. He says the program is "significantly likely" to violate the Fourth

Amendment which addresses protection against unreasonable searches (Dec. 16). Just days after Judge Leon's ruling, an advisory panel commissioned by President Obama releases a 300-page report that recommends 46 changes to the NSA surveillance program (Dec 18).

2014 – (January 1) Obamacare, the Affordable Care Act, goes into effect for millions of Americans, the largest expansion of the social welfare state in decades. Over 7.3 million join the system, some due to cancellations of existing healthcare policies; others due to subsidies provided by the government. Premiums for policies see large increases due to expansion. (February 26) Only days after hosting the Winter Olympic Games in Sochi, Russia, the Russian Federation annexes the Ukrainian territory of Crimea, causing widespread condemnation, a temporary suspension of Russia from the G8, and limited sanctions by the United States. Russian expansionism becomes a topic for the first time since the end of the Cold War in 1989. (June 5) Rise of ISIS in a large amount of territory in western Syria and northern Iraq cause western nations to confront another round of Islamic fundamentalism. United States and some allies begin campaign to degrade their effectiveness with a bombing campaign on September 22. (September 30) First case of Ebola is certified in the United States, an outcome of travel from the country of Liberia and West Africa where the virus has spread to 22,000 people and killed 9,000. (November 4) Midterm elections see large increase in Republican lawmakers with expansion of their majority to 247 seats in the House of Representatives and the taking over of the majority in the Senate with 54 seats. This will cause the Obama administration to deal with a Congress now controlled by the other party for the final two years of his term. Trayvon Martin race riots occur nationwide. Ferguson race riots (Michael Brown) erupt in St. Louis, Missouri, and nationwide. Eric Garner race riots take place in Staten Island, New

York, and nationwide. Ferguson race riots (Michael Brown) erupt in St. Louis, Missouri, and nationwide. Two policemen are assassinated (racially inspired) in Brooklyn, New York.

2015 – (June 6) American Pharoah becomes the first horse in thirty-seven years to win the Triple Crown of horse racing with his victory in the Belmont Stakes. (June 16) Billionaire businessman Donald Trump joins a crowded field of Republican candidates seeking the nomination for President in 2016 and almost immediately rises to the top of the polls on a populist message, surprising pundits and critics. Expected frontrunner on the Democratic side, Hillary Clinton, takes quick lead in the polls. (July 20) Full diplomatic relations are reestablished between the United States and Cuba for the first time in fifty-four years. (September 22) Pope Francis makes his first visit to the United States, holding services in Washington, New York City, and Philadelphia. This was the first papal visit to the U.S.A. since Pope Benedict XVI in 2008 and only the fourth pope to ever visit the United States. (December 2) Islamic Terrorist inspired act in San Bernadino, California kills fourteen and follows a brutal attack against citizens in Paris in November. These attacks and others are fueled by the continual rise of ISIS in Syria, Iraq, and other countries around the world.

2016 – This year was dominated by increased world Muslim terror attacks and the presidential elections.

This was a pivotal year for the United States of America; Socialism, Constitutional Republic or Civil War. Socialism has had 50 plus years to establish itself in the Nation.

Per the 2016 election our Nation was given a reprieve to reverse the Socialist Movement by electing a Conservative Populist President with a mandate in Congress.

The Trump Presidency reinforced the reality that taking our Nation back from the Socialist Democrats is going to be a long, difficult process. The Globalists and Socialists formed a movement during his presidency called the "Resistance" which sought to impeach him and resist all of his election promises and programs. The Constitution, the Bill of Rights and the Ten Commandments were all being trampled on by the Socialist Democrats. As predicted previously, they have had 50 plus years to slither into all areas of our Nation, the fight will be difficult.

2020 -- This was also a very important election in the history of our Nation. The Socialists (Biden) were re-elected in a very suspect election process and we still do not know if our Nation will be a Constitutional Republic, a Socialist State or a Nation fighting its second Civil War.

God Help us!

2022 and 2024 -- We will know the future of our country after these two elections. American patriots must take the country back in the 2022 Congressional Election and the 2024 Presidential Election or our Constitutional Republic falls!

Made in the USA
Las Vegas, NV
06 January 2022

40559633R10131